house of fields

house of fields

memories of a rural education

ANNE-MARIE OOMEN

Wayne State University Press Detroit

Manufactured in the United States of America.

10 09 08 07 06   5 4 3 2 1

Library of Congress Cataloging-in-Publication Data

Oomen, Anne-Marie.
House of fields : memories of a rural education / Anne-Marie Oomen.
p. cm. — (Great Lakes books)
ISBN 0-8143-3285-4 (pbk. : alk. paper)
1. Oomen, Anne-Marie—Childhood and youth. 2. Oomen, Anne-Marie—Family.
3. Country life—Michigan—Oceana County—History—20th century. 4. Farm life—Michigan—Oceana County—History—20th century. 5. Education, Rural—Michigan—Oceana County—History—20th century. 6. Oceana County (Mich.)—Social life and customs—20th century. 7. Oceana County (Mich.)—Biography. 8. Girls—Michigan—Oceana County—Biography. 9. Farmers—Michigan—Oceana County—Biography. I. Title.
F572.O3O57 2006
977.4'59043092—dc22
[B]
2006021648

Except for the author's immediate family and general references to families in the region, the names of all individuals in this book have been changed.

∞

Designed and typeset by Maya Rhodes
Composed in Bembo

To my father and mother,
who believed so passionately in the value of education,
but particularly my mother, who, more than anyone else,
put up with the child who was always running heedlessly forward,
if not in body, in mind.

I have been permanently shaped—and am still held fast—by landscapes that exist in memory alone, though this makes them no less real when they come to me in dreams, when fragments are triggered by a random fact. . . .

It doesn't take much—a look, a phrase—and suddenly I'm a child once more, running hard and fast down a narrow dirt road. . . . Yet there's no sense, as I run, that I'm recreating something, repainting this landscape as if by numbers, filling in color and sound. I'm simply *here,* I'm *home,* and any return to the present will be informed by what I've seen.

—A. Manette Ansay, *Limbo: A Memoir*

CONTENTS

ACKNOWLEDGMENTS

I am forever indebted to all those at Wayne State University Press who have helped bring this book to fruition, especially Annie Martin, acquisitions editor, for continuing to believe in and support my work, and to her reviewers who helped me understand the manuscript's final revision. My thanks to *Traverse: Northern Michigan's Magazine* and its affiliated magazine, *Northern Home,* for early publication of some of these essays, and to Norm and Jacob Wheeler at the *Glen Arbor Sun* for the same. Much appreciation to my colleagues at Interlochen Arts Academy, particularly Jack Driscoll and Mike Delp, for helpful conversations regarding some of the essays and the process of revision. Thanks to Aaron Stander and the gang at Michigan Writers for real encouragement, and to the sauna family for always being present to the story. A word of recogition to Mimi Wheeler and Grocer's Daughter Chocolates, without which I couldn't have written a page. Thank you to my friends, who somehow continue to understand what it means to write. My loving and eternal thanks to my husband, David Early, for building the Think House (where I write) and chopping the wood that keeps it warm, for making it all possible, and for putting up with such a strange and intense process. My sincerest gratitude to my parents, John and Ruth Oomen, and my siblings, Tom, Rick, Marijo, and Pat, for putting up with me, period, and for letting me put the writing first.

PROLOGUE: THE HOUSE

The house I grew up in is filled with the worn hands and weathered faces of my people, with secondhand furniture, ordinary dreams. The place is scented with smoky ham, chicken fat, wet laundry, old shoes, hardworking bodies. The linoleum floors, with their green-and-white squares, echo the grid of the fields around them. In this house the oatmeal is stirred, eggs fried, roasts roasted, and vegetables boiled to within an inch of their pulpy lives. There is the oak table, its grain sticky with syrup or ketchup or spit or tears or intermittent tender talk. There is the cool living room with its blue 1950s sofa and its ornate but dog-scratched door swinging open onto the porch of stone, an eye to the yard and road and world beyond. And there is that wide open staircase to the second floor, an odd elegance against the chipped cup of our existence.

This house embodies our contradictions: great heart and poor soil; inventive spirit and stoic acceptance of all things terrible; some secrets caught tightly at the corner of the mouth set against hands warm enough to warm the cold.

Look out any window of the Oomen farmhouse and the fields and orchards of Oceana County stretch open like hands until they run smack
into Lake Michigan, the big, west water that assures the county's one
blessing—a microclimate that keeps our springtimes cool and our au-
tumns warm. South of our village of Crystal Valley and far enough inland
to make that promise unreliable is this place called the Oomen Farm,
some two hundred acres knuckled with low hills of green corn, dusty
hay, leggy asparagus, wild pasture. There, a scattering of buildings anchor
our farm like stones holding down paper in the wind: workshop, granary,
corn crib, chicken coop, little barns, and big barns. Of all the buildings
that weight our lives and keep everything from flying out from the animal and machine forces, the big barn is most important. From the barn,
pipelines of activity, like arteries and veins, take in and pump out the
work of cows, chickens, pigs, tractors, combines, ordinary tools, and great
work.

A heart then.

But there is also that house. With its windows and porches, it sits
apart, as frayed as a tired woman. The dwelling, with its white clapboard
peeling and its roof shingles blotched and patched with tar, is perched on
a low western slope. That said, the ridgeline holds steady as a taut chalk
line. Of all the buildings, it is the least important structure. Justifiably,
farmers will fix a fence line before they will fix the screen door. They
will save a calf before they will caulk windows against winter. In this
worn, often broken space rests another core. But not the heart. For lack
of a better metaphor, and at risk of sentiment, call this core a soul.

On farms, souls are dispensable. The heart is not. A heart can be
eaten after all, the soul cannot. On our farm, among the whirling, thudding motion of tractors, pickups, muddy fields, and poor harvests, our
family spirit lives and breathes in that worn farmhouse. Our household
is a restless one, molded by immigration only one generation earlier, by
the ambition that rises from ordinary oppression, by the undeniable and
contradictory gods of fields and weather. It is where we sleep, wake, eat,
and find ourselves called out by the hard ways of the crops we grow and
by the world outside the county that always seems different from us and
therefore we do not entirely trust.

That farmhouse is where my four siblings—Tom, Rick, Marijo, Patti—and I, Anne or Annie, depending on the whim of the year—received our first education. The earliest lessons are plain—bitter coffee, canned peaches, musty sheets, torn screens, curtains faded with sunlight. At the house's thin threshold and smudged windows, we learned not only the work of our lives but also the lives of the people who lived before: Grandma Julia Van Agtmeal, who came here to live for a decade before she fell on the cement step of the wood room and my mother could not lift her; Grandma Josephine Oomen, who died in my parents' bedroom; Grandpa Henry Oomen who, when he finally left the fields, wondered where his son and his supper were, though both were right in front of him. As we grew older, the living lessons stemmed also from whole families of cousins: Van Agtmeals, Shields, Coffees, the other Oomens; or foster children, Bobbie, Matt; or neighbors, Raymond and Mabel, Butler and Evelyn, Marilyn and Walt; or dogs and cats: Duke, Dutch, Biscuit, Christmas; even calves in the living room—all entered the canon of our lives and taught the rules of shelter and endurance, common and necessary as mud.

It is our house, the actual house, that is an anomaly. For it is a bigger house than most and—a word foreign to farm culture—*beautiful.* The house where I am always a girl has four porches, one of stone. An east kitchen with a paneled pantry runs the length of the house. A solid sliding pocket door with oak panels separates the first parlor and the old dining room, which features built-in linen drawers. The bedrooms have real closets hung with solid doors. The stain on all the wood is warm cherry. The glass in the front doors is frosted with swirling floral designs. On sunny days, the big front windows, graced with small panels of beveled glass, toss tiny rainbows across turn-of-the-century wallpaper.

Despite these signatures of affluence, by the time my parents, John Cornelius Oomen and Ruth Jean Van Agtmeal, purchase it in the late 1940s, after my father returned from World War II a quieter man, the house has moldered. A cistern in the attic has leaked through the ceilings, the inefficient wood stove has sooted every corner, the kitchen floor is rotting, the lath and horsehair walls invite the cold through cracks

Ruth Oomen and daughter Anne-Marie

as wide as cutlery, the basement stinks with damp. Still, the surviving touches of grace counteract the world of war and Depression they have survived. My mother likes it, perhaps because the glimmers of past affluence remind her of her brief years as a governess for a banker family in Lake Forest, Illinois. Perhaps my father likes it because they can purchase it from his father who had himself purchased it years earlier—the finances will be simpler. But when I think of them, I like to imagine their choice to live in this house springs from an aesthetic they rarely otherwise acknowledge: that they love its tattered beauty.

Of that beauty, one feature outclasses all others—a staircase of such unusual proportions and detail it is a mystery. This is not a typical farmhouse stairway enclosed with unfinished walls and crooked steps that rise to badly plastered upper rooms. This is an open staircase made of dark maple and oak. The wood is nubbed with delicate rows of tiny carved beads. The banisters stand thick and four-cornered, ornate with newel detail. It has an open landing with a high window that pours morning light down onto the steps. The baluster that rims the upper hall provides a view of the living room. At the bottom, beneath the steps, a small shelf holds a handful of books: classic fairy tales, the Bible, a missal. The staircase represents another world, moneyed and finished in a way a farm never is. More than any other part, that stairway—conduit of motion—is the center of the house.

There, dirty-socked Tom and Rick patter their first wars; Marijo and Patti dance up in slips and step down in the Easter dresses of girlhood. Rick, as a young man, thuds up to grab a clean tee shirt before meeting his girl; a budding Marijo plods down to whisper to our mother that she has her first period. We five bound, skip, rush, and trip to catch the impatient yellow busses of our mornings. Our heels land hard, grilling the steps with two hundred plus footfalls each morning. The wood at the center of the tread grays and thins with wear until the year my mother finds money for carpet, which covers the old wood and softens our rough impact. Decades later a daughter-in-law yanks up the old rug to discover the grain, still straight and true between the tacking strips, a strength that has held the repeated shock of four generations. Every important childhood photo, from first doll to last prom, is taken on those steps.

What I learn is that if I stop and sink onto a step, I can blend into the stacked laundry waiting to be carried up. I can peer quietly through the spindles in the dark, watch siblings heckle on the couch, listen to an adult inform of sudden death, hear all their talk. I can listen to my mother's voice rising from the kitchen like the scent of complicated soup. From there I learn who is in trouble, who is praised. I can plan, coming down those stairs, what to say in the other rooms where the living takes place. If the house proper is the site of our first education, the staircase is the secret library, the place where knowledge is garnered. That staircase is the site of connection, an architecture open and rising, contrasting to the flat burn and demand of fields. A place of transition. The heart of the soul?

I am there, halfway up the first flight, hiding behind the spindles. For all my hunger for attention, the only way I ever learn what my beloved adults do not want me to know is by sitting inside the emptiness of that staircase. They forget me then. On the day I learn the story of our house, they are in the living room below, gathered and sated after Sunday ham. My father, Grandpa Henry, Great Aunt Mary Willumen, Grandpa Joe Van Agtmeal and Grandma Julia, perhaps Aunts Minnie and Catherine from Chicago, any number of cousins lean and slouch on chairs that look like they've sat in a hard rain. In a few minutes my mother, who wants me to do dishes so that the visiting adults will know I am being taught to work, will call from the kitchen. I have only this little box of time before she discovers me.

It is then that I hear the story.

My Aunt Catherine's voice begins. Or it may have been Grandpa Henry, the one who would know. Let's say it was his voice, for there is something important about having learned it from an elder. Let's say they are talking about the changes my mother will make, how she wants to remodel the house now that there is a little money. She has just entered the room with Aunt Minnie, talking about knocking down the walls between the kitchen and the dining room to make one big family room. She has seen these rooms in *Better Homes and Gardens.*

"Careful of those walls," Grandpa Henry says.

"We know which ones are bearing," she tells him, wiping her hands on a dishtowel. He has a huge mustache that gives him an authority she does not always understand. She throws the towel over her shoulder.

Tom, my younger brother, asks, "What's a bear wall?"

My dad speaks the correction quietly so we will remember, "A bearing wall holds up something else. It needs support. Can't change bearing walls. Can't let them bear anything but what they was meant to."

"Not what I mean," my grandfather interrupts, licking his fork for the last crumbs of cobbler. "This house wasn't the first."

There is a small lake of silence. Grandpa's mustache twitches. "Old Kelly told me. Their people built this house around another house."

My mother makes a sound that means she suspects a lie, then changes her mind. "Another house?"

Grandpa nods, "They left a small one standing inside. Lived in it while they finished. You watch the walls, maybe something of the first house got used over."

My mother sighs—another ghost to battle when she wants to be more modern, to make things nice. I sit on the steps. I run my fingers along the beads of the banister, counting quietly, thinking about this new idea. How did it work? Like nesting bowls? Onions? Did they build tall walls around short ones? When they took it down, did the men pass studs out through windows? Did they leave anything?

I am the only one of the siblings who can remember the original floor plan of the farmhouse today. I think the second parlor, which became the dining room, is large enough to have surrounded a small shack. Thinking of this house I become that little girl again. I stare through the spindles down at my grandfather who has just told a story that is rippling out like a flood in a low field. I look at this family, at their hands hard as stone and calloused as paws. The light writes the old words of loyalty and reliability all over their faces. They do not think about the empty or secret places. I am trying to see this hidden and lost house, trying to see something even older than our farmhouse, to see how it was passed through, how we pass through it even now.

A house within a house.

I look with new eyes at the walls. What will we find when we pull down the old striped paper and knock the plaster from the lath? What will my mother discover, shaking her head, that she will hold in her hands? I am trapped in the unfinished thing, in what this half story does. I have been given something that needs to be completed, something infused with surprise, like being in the center of a field with all that space around.

I sit on the staircase and listen for the stories, the ones from the mouths of my family, from the salt-of-the-earth grandparents, the chatty aunts, the solid father who sometimes reads books late at night, the four siblings angling for love and someone to pitch that baseball. In a little while my mother will find me and ask, with a small tension in her voice, to come and do dishes with her. I will but not willingly. I want to be on the staircase, looking over these folks, listening. I want the stories, to hear what is unsaid as much as what is said. I want to learn how it works, one thing inside another, some strut of meaning to be discovered and passed out. It is the beginning, that story of the house inside a house, anchored by the long and sustaining fields.

UNCLE JOHN

His was my first clear death.

Before Grandpa Joe, before my aunt's blue baby, before the cousin with cancer, before the elders began to die—one a year for a decade or so—his was the death that shaped death. First death is like hard rain in a gulley; it washes out something that can never be replaced. And the person who delivers the message of death is something too in the roles that shape our lives. It was my mother who told us; it would be she who would always tell us.

It starts in my parents' bedroom. We never wander into that space. We are called there or taken there if we are sick. It is a "sacred" room, though we do not know that language yet. That Christmas morning when my mother calls all three of us older ones to her bed, we already sense this is not about the baby Jesus or Santa Claus or even about getting ready for morning Mass. She is tender. She puts her arms around us and holds each of us. She tells us in quiet words that Uncle John has gone to heaven. At first, there is confusion among the bedcovers, a trying-to-figure-something-out rippling that slowly stills itself like water in a bowl. We look at her, listening to the silences between her words. At last we know. My brothers cry, especially Tom, who played cards with this fierce-eyed man. Uncle John was a man kinder to boys than girls, and Tom and Rick know something has ended for them. But for me it is the change on people's faces, how their mouths tremble like a sheet of rain, then harden to stone. It is my mother's quiet voice set against her strong hands fumbling with the ragged edge of the blanket.

She sits on the bed at Christmastime, which is always full of happy bustle underpinned with worry about money. She sits. My father some-times sits like this, but my mother? So seldom that it is hard to know her like this. She should be standing in a rush, brushing down her jeans or skirt, looking toward the kitchen, the turkey or ham, the green beans, the diapers, anything but this sitting still, touching the edge of a blanket as if it were a broken fence line. She is not like this. And for all the times I have wanted to sit with her, it has always been for the clear window into her being, not this fumbling. What is happening?

It is about this thing called death.

Over the next few days, it becomes about Uncle John's body in the thing called a coffin with its white satin lining and the way his beard juts up in a kind of argument with the world. It is the long litanies for the dead mingling with stories. The men tell proud memories of how he prayed and farmed, quieter ones of how he held on to money. The women shake their heads at his temper, then hold their mouths and make their breath come out slow. For me, this death becomes my earliest story. My mother tells me not to ask questions, but I put it together by sitting on the staircase and listening. I hear the parts she tells the others before they cannot talk anymore because the tears wash over them and hollow them out.

The way I save myself from being washed away is through the story I make up.

Christmas midnight Mass. Like all the children I grew up with, I know the carols. I know how the candles glow, their points of light. Around the crèche, six full-sized pine trees from Mr. Dean's farm. The poinsettias, all the way from Mexico. Teardrop bulbs strung in red, green, and blue hover as too-near stars made close-up to show us that even the debris of the universe came to the manger. The choir has sung a long High Mass, and now the line for Communion is long too, a human chain lumbering forward down the center aisle. Here the big and thin and small men lift their heads and are fed the thing called a Host.

Uncle John also steps into place before the priest. Maybe he thinks it is cold in the church, this man who never needed much heat. He answers the priest, his *amen* as flat as it should be. He closes his mouth around the wafer, turns, and faces back toward the side aisle, toward the pew on the east where he and Mary have sat for decades. It is that dark pew where he will kneel and cover his head and let his thoughts drift a little. He turns toward it, ignoring the chill running through his arms. He is reaching for the dark curve of the pew when the cold knifes so hard through him that his lungs contract, balloons deflating. He feels himself stumble, a man who never stumbles, whose temper and temperament will not let him, but here he is, stumbling into the kind of pain that blurs the candles and makes the distant hymn wheeze around the edges. He feels the arms of other men, good men, though he would push them away if he could. Men with the Host still melting on their tongues should not have to help him—he just has to catch his breath, take it back from this sharp vacuum. But when he tries to shrug them off his legs buckle, the whole season loosens its colors and lets them go free in this so-cold air. They turn bright, then brighter, and the night, the holy night, opens in his bowels. Even as his body is lowered, I imagine the whispered call that goes out among the pews. Nieces, nephews, old friends slip from their places to the back aisle. With Aunt Mary looking on, he dies in his church.

Maybe none of this is true.

Except this is the story I make from the remnants of what they will tell me. Over time, I run the scene so many times in my head that it becomes familiar in its textures, a picture I recognize as though I had been there. It becomes more real because it is unfinished.

Nothing can match first death. Nothing can equal death in any case—its surprise, intrigue, mystery, the hands and faces of it.

But even as the story evolves, the other thing rises, a cold stone in the surface of a springtime field. When I think about that time, that first death and funeral, it is coupled with that other memory, the one I cannot change, my mother on the bed before she gets up and goes to talk to people, that image of her tucked into herself. In all the funerals that follow, I will see it again and again. I will go back and touch, like a tongue worrying a sore tooth, these deaths that actually stopped her busy, competent hands. I will imagine her hands in work, the way they move like the strong song of an engine through days, the cycle of fields and gardens, how they enact a dance of tasks that we rely on utterly. Through them the world of my girlhood is whole. When her hands are still, it is not like stillness at all but something fearful, something "other" coming loose and falling. Like the angels in the Christmas story, she is dangerous and laced with love, her voice a dark tenderness like wings stilled, her hands betraying her fears.

DYNAMITE

For a long time it lives in the granary and we don't know about it. Or rather, we know about the heavy box with peeling paper wrap, red lettering, and the skull and crossbones on the outside, but we don't know what it holds. We stare at the box when we play in the wheat bins, but we have been warned never to touch it in such serious tones that even Tom and Rick, "the boys," are not tempted. Still, it is alive with our looking, our thorny interest.

Over breakfast one morning, my father says he must blow it up.

"Blow what up?" Tom is hopping from one foot to the other, his elbows sticking out like flapping chicken wings. Rick is quiet like he is, watching from his chair. The little girls, Marijo and Patti, are still asleep.

My mother has put her cup down with a sharp click.

My father explains, "To get rid of it."

Tom asks, "Can we do like they do in the movies? Can we blow up the chicken coop?"

My father sighs. He is looking at my mother. "I've been reading. The stuff is old. Unstable. It could be dangerous."

"Unstable?" she asks.

"Nitroglycerin in that form is supposed to be turned every month. I didn't know that. I've never done it." His uncertainty hovers crowlike over the table.

"You're saying it could go off at any time?"

"Not if we get rid of it."

"It's been in the granary since you cleared the pasture." My mother lifts her cup, blows on her coffee, and silently counts the years.

"You blew up something?" Tom, putting it together, is frantic that he might have missed something. He is kneeling on his chair, his hands on top of his head.

"We blew up some ditches. Didn't use it all." My father stares at his eggs.

"How many are left?" My mother's voice is too light. The number will make the threat into something she can measure.

"Half a box," he says. She waits. He rubs his hand on the back of his head and does not look at her. "Fifty or so."

She gasps.

I don't know how many fifty is, but the sound of her breath tells me it is a lot. And then there are these new words: *explode, unstable. Night or glisten.* They sound like what they must mean. Something unexpected.

When it becomes clear that nothing will be blown up except the dynamite itself, Tom and Rick settle for following my father, trailing at his pockets and underfoot until his patience is worn out. My mother has tried every argument and has made every suggestion for other ways to be rid of it, but my father says no one else can do it, and it must be done. When the time comes, my father tells all of us to stay at the house. My brothers are appalled that they cannot be with him. They wiggle like puppies, but our mother forbids them from *taking one step* off the back porch. From the porch, we can see across the barnyards to the granary and the fields beyond. Here, we are protected.

We watch the story unfold.

He lifts and places a long piece of wood over the steps to the granary to make a ramp. He pushes the big wooden slider door to the side and climbs into the building. My mother, watching, puts a hand over her mouth. When it takes a long time for him to come out, she looks away and stares down at some dog shit piled along the edge of the yard. My mother doesn't look away from anything.

When my father comes back into the light, he is holding the box with the red letters in front of him, a little away from his body. He walks differently than I have ever seen him walk, like cold syrup from a spilled bottle. He walks away from the buildings—the barns, workshop, the chicken coop. Stopping now and then to hold very still, he climbs the east hill. He places his feet so carefully that I think they are like the cars in a choo-choo train, one after another, alike and evenly spaced as days, until he disappears like something sinking on the other side of the hill. My mother makes a rough cluck in her throat. Without her anchor of steadiness, a gnawing of worry grows in us. Unable to sit still on the steps for more than a few seconds, we wiggle in and out of the shadows on the porch, first at the railings, then the gray clapboarding, then swinging on the post and peeling its shards of old paint until she speaks sharply to *stop it*. We shift our gaze from her face to the hill and back to her face. After a while something in it loosens, a shoelace coming free of its knot. My father appears, rising like a dark ghost over the hill's crest, his body silhouetted against the sky. But now he walks in a natural pace down the hill and turns toward the house. My mother breathes.

"Did it go off?" Tom looks as though he is about to wail. Rick is biting his lower lip.

"Not yet," my mother whispers.

My father does not speak with us. His face is still thinking, focused on what he must do. He comes to the house swiftly, walking with quick, hard steps. He bangs down the rickety steps to the basement and rummages around. When he climbs up the rough steps, he is carrying his rifle and a small box of shells.

My mother looks at him.

"It's the only way I can think of," he says to her and leaves again, the rifle in the crook of his elbow.

"Yer gonna shoot it?" Tom asks, delight pouring from every cell. Rick smiles.

We move as one body to the porch rail to track his movements. Again, he crosses the barnyards, leaves the circle of buildings, climbs to the crest, and at the very top of the hill but still in full view, he kneels, loads the gun slowly, then lowers himself to his belly. He is so low in the grasses that the rifle, extended before him as he aims, looks like the stinger of a mosquito. Then he shimmies back, down from the highest point. Watching how he is using the hill to protect himself, my hands turn cold. I look at my mother. Again, she is looking down, her mouth calm, as though there were something of great interest growing between the boards in the porch.

At the first sound, everyone looks at one another. But it is merely a gunshot, a sound that, because we've lived among hunters and hunting from the time we could crawl, we know. Despite its power, it is familiar. It does not frighten us.

"He missed," my brother says, a little disgusted. Rick shakes his head and scuffs the dirt below the lowest step.

"It's hard at that angle," my mother tells him. But when he misses a second time, she makes a tisking sound, as though she would like to scold someone who has annoyed her. Her mouth knots up again, her expression turns tight and too quiet.

My hands ache. I pull the hem of my tee shirt and stick my thumb into my mouth. My mother speaks her mind; she says when something is not right. And if she is not doing that now, what is wrong?

Fifty sticks of dynamite.

The explosion, when it comes, makes the sharp pop of the rifle seem like a sound from a toy. This sound is lightning and thunder at exactly the same moment, a small and ugly sun, hard and fast, scarring the mind. It is bigger than any other sound in our small lives. It rolls down the hillsides, bangs against the barns and sheds, and bounces off everything, leaving it raw as skin scraped clean. It is night collapsed into itself, stars blinking on and off at once. I hear it, we all hear it, and there is nothing that can take it back. Dust and smoke fly up and out like gray fireworks, then drop into a slow cloud down the hill.

My father lies in the grass for so long that my mother makes a motion like an animal tied to something it cannot get away from. Her body jerks toward him, then back, holding itself in some cage. At last, he pushes himself up on all fours, rises to his knees, lifts the rifle, stands, dusts off his arms, scuffs in the dirt, unloads the gun, and disappears over the crest. For the first time since the task began, we are still. A stream of dark smoke rises and rises. Finally, for the second time, he appears above the crest. He gestures that it is okay for us to come. My brothers leap like pebbles shot from rubber slingshots.

I turn to see my mother, her face white, looking up at the kitchen window. A single crack slithers all the way across the clear glass, dividing it like a cut from a knife. It breaks the reflection of the fields in two. I look away. Then I too am running, with wild curiosity, to see this thing that was big enough to change the world. I want to tell my father that it was a good story.

When my mother and I reach the hilltop and look down the slope, my brothers are running around the hole. They have already been stopped from climbing into it because it is, my father says, "hot as hell."

"As hell," Tom says, his voice big.

I look down into a gray hole that smells like metal that's too hot. The grass all around is singed black for several feet. Here and there tiny flames pop up out of nowhere. My father walks around and around, stepping on burned grass, twisting his boot hard onto these places. He asks my mother to bring the water bucket. He tells us to look and then move away until it all cools down. I step close, sniffing the bitterness that stings and holding my breath as I realize how big the hole is. The hole could fit my mother and me, my father, and Tom and Rick. It could fit Marijo and Patti too—though Patti is too small to walk—plus maybe even my bigger cousins, Eddy Jo, Harry, Mike, Teddy, and Kathy. I stand with my body open, thinking how many of my family could climb into it and not ever fill it. But what makes me feel sick—even as I am trying to figure out how many people it could hold—is how empty it is. Something that was our own dirt—solid, steady as a field—is now like a hot, gray bowl. The hole is empty, a mouth that needs to be filled and can never be filled. As though it had eaten itself. There was earth and now there is not. It scares me more than the cracked window.

When I look at my father, I see that he is too quiet. I think about the sound, how it came to us bigger than anything real, how it made emptiness, not the good kind where you can sit in it and listen to the outside world, but a new kind, the kind that would hurt you if you stayed inside it too long. You would never be able to hear anything in a hole like that. You would never fill it with anything, people or words, because it is the kind of empty that—yes, I know this now—could kill you. I look hard at my father's face, now deep red as though he has been in the sun too long. I realize he has no eyebrows.

House of School

Dressed in a pretty white blouse and a plaid jumper, I stand in front of our stone front porch and smile. My mother snaps the picture, stills the moment, the brink of my entering another house. She knows this day means more than the jumper, more than the small smile. She takes a picture to hold the day, to make it more like a stone in the porch, solid as that, so when I look at this picture I can say this was me on my first day of school.

So it will be real.

But the picture does not exist yet; it is in the box camera, and to me the farmhouse behind me is the only solid thing. My first house. That house is real. My little brothers and sisters, somewhere in those rooms, are surely real with their noise like constantly running water. Even my mother is more there than I am, in the undertone to everything in that picture, the choice of fabric, her will tangible behind the picture she takes with a small camera. Everything else is tentative: the light, the spirea bushes, me limpid and plaid, not quite in focus.

I stand still and smile small as a first lie. I stand still in the spirea and maple shadows long after the picture is taken and she has slid the camera back into its case, snapped it shut, and placed it on the steps. Now I am supposed to leave her, leave the house and walk down the drive to this new place. I think about it for so long that I do not hear her when she returns to stand beside me.

The truth is, I am sure I will get lost on the way to the square building that is, everyone tells me, just *down the road*. Although I can see it from the end of our driveway, a large white shoebox with a cap they call a belfry, I am afraid I won't know where I am in that place *just south of here* on our gravel road, bordered by burdock and tiger lilies. I look up at her. She is staring too, down the road, as though she could see to the end of it.

I look too.

I try to look the way she looks, with long-seeing eyes. The road widens and runs beyond our yard and barns and fields. The morning is sunny and September cool. I notice other children already walking, strolling, or half-running down the road toward the school. Although I do not know all of them, my mother does. She knows them from living a long time in one place. She knows the French Canadian boy by the shape of his nose; the boy with a limp from a PTO accident years ago; sometimes she knows them by the smell from their shoes, the sour that announces a dairy farm, the sickly sweet that says fruit work. She names them for me as they pass the house. Johnny. Allen. Judy. Merton. Donny. Theresa. George. The names help me fit them into the world. Some look up as we stand on the edge of the yard, some wave in that soft hesitation made by rural people when they are unsure of rules. They stare at me. I offer a smile, but when I should step forward my feet do not move. I stick my thumb in my mouth and watch.

Dust rises from their dark work shoes. The girls laugh at each other, their bodies buttoned-up in cotton and summer-brown skin. The big boys hoot and call; some carry bats across their shoulders. They do not stand and watch from some yard. My mother nudges my shoulder, stops when still I do not move, and makes a sound with her breath that means she has changed her mind. She takes my hand. Her fingers are as hard as bread left out too long, but warm. She leads me away from our house, toward the road, toward this other house. She will walk with me to school after all.

The bell in the green belfry sounds out like church, but brighter, quicker. We join the line of bodies. From Sugar Hill to the south, from Smith's Corners to the north, we all walk. I ask why we don't take the car. My mother says schools are meant to be walked to—they are close to everyone's house. Still, a rusty car passes us and drops off two kids from the shantytown. But we walk, now among them, and as we do I watch the school come closer, changing like a season. I am surprised it is not as long a road as her eyes had said. We turn into the two-track driveway, stepping from gravel to thin grass to worn path. We climb wide cement stairs to a porch where some kids sit, eating their sack lunches for breakfast. We pass into the scuffling coolness of the mudroom where the plank floors are dark with wear.

We stop at the door propped open with a stick and stare in.

The square green room is high-ceilinged, mapped with water stains. Long chains wrapped with frayed wire drop four plain lightbulbs from the tin ceiling so they hover over the desks like eggs. The south light falling through tall double-hung windows onto the floor is so bright I can see dust motes swirling in the air like tiny lightning bugs. The wooden desks are set one in front of the other in three rows. Each desk connects so that the front of one holds the seat of the next one. The spaces between the rows are uneven, but the squareness of things is alive. Everything, even the light splashed on the floors, is old yet still has sharp corners.

At the head of the room the largest desk I have ever seen sits solid as dark rock. Chairs of all sizes, some that fold up, form a half circle. And there, stretching across the entire front of the room, is a blackboard. One panel has white lines on which a name is written. I cannot read, but I recognize how names look. Is it the teacher's name? I like names. They answer the question of who you are. Names make me feel as if there is a way to connect things, like the way the desks are connected.

All the desks in the room lean toward the blackboard, which is full of things that have not happened yet. The whole room is like that, full of something that will happen to me, but I do not know what it will be. The other children are filing in, pushing around us, looking into desks and speaking with big voices. The room already smells like skin too long in the sun. We stand, a little wobbly, at the threshold that will take us into the room.

I look up at my mother. She has the same expression she gets when she looks at the Sears catalog. She is nodding at the girls with their first-day-of-school dresses, at the boys in freshly washed coveralls and worn shoes. Even the big boys are here, the ones who could work at home. I am drawn to their voices. They talk about baseball. They call the players by name as if they were friends, especially someone named Al Kaline, who is a Tiger. That's our team. My father listens to the games on Sunday afternoon radio. He has told me the team was named after the tiger because it is strong and can win. The boys' voices are as big as machines.

I want her to talk to me. I want someone to say my name the way the boys say the names of the players. I want to go into the room, but my small feet can't seem to make the step.

"Does it have a name?" I am trying for something.

"What?"

"The school?"

"Kelly School," she answers. Now she is looking at the book-shelves.

"Why?" If a baseball team is named for a tiger because the tiger can win, does the school being named Kelly mean something?

My mother sighs. *Why* is my most often asked question. Although she is tired of it, she answers. "The school is named after the family who built our house. Who owned the land. Before Grandpa Henry came from Holland, the Kellys gave the land for the school building. It's named for them. We know the family."

I know people can be named after other people, because I have aunts named after grandmothers. But for a place to be named after people is new to me. This place, this not-our-house-not-our-barn, this schoolhouse, square and plain with its bell and mudroom and wide blackboard, is named after people my mother knows like the boys know the baseball players. I lean against her. She pulls her gaze away from the room, looks at me, and smiles her own small smile. There is something old in it, like my grandmother's smile, like mist rising from a wet field on a warm day.

With my mother at my side, I step up into the room with the high ceilings, the tall windows, and the giant beetle of an oil furnace crouching in the corner. We walk side by side toward the front of the room. I touch the wrought-iron filigree that holds the desks together, running my short fingers over the metal designs that remind me of the fairy-tale pictures.

In a spray of southern light let down by a tall window, my mother lets go of my hand. When she leaves, moving so quietly I know it is on purpose, I pretend not to notice because I think that is how it should go. I look at the teacher, this woman who has a voice nothing like my mother's, who seems more like a busy stranger. I do not cry. I want to like it, this school. I want it to happen so much that my small itches about being without my mother are already hidden by the wanting. Still, I stay quiet until my name is called. The teacher points to a small desk with carvings all over the top. I slide into the seat. My hands, roving the desk, trace the carvings. These are names. Whose names?

The light comes in and falls on the desks, bookshelves, floor. It spills onto the old shoes and wool socks. Above, the blackboard hovers, full of its unwritten promise. All of us, smelling of dirt and home-fried eggs, shift into our seats like a settling flock. My body explores it all: this desk, this sitting here, this being in school. This being without my mother. In that first simple loneliness, this house comes into focus and I am in it. If I sit in the desk long enough, I believe my name will appear with all the others.

Big Words, Little Words

My mother has scraped the remains of the chicken onto the big serving plate before clearing the table. The bones are heaped like pink and gray twigs, picked clean of bark, stacked for burning.

"That's what the chickens would look like if we coulda blown up the coop." Tom is still imagining what it would be like to blow up something. He stuffs more bread into his mouth. "I bet Granpa Joe blew stuff up." We have all heard stories of my Grandpa Joe Van Agtmeal in what they call the Great War. "I bet he knows. He shoulda wrote it down. In secret codes." He has a way of speaking like a motor that runs, stops, runs again.

My mother says, "Grandpa Joe couldn't write. Or read." A moment of silence like a small round ball sits among us. She bends to wipe Marijo's face. I feel sadness in her voice and another sound like hiding under covers at night.

"Coud-unt?" Tom makes the word like the two parts of an egg being cracked open—crack and plop. "But you got old letters. From that war." I remember the thin, folded paper. Little Patti fusses, awake from her nap. I pull her onto my lap so that my mother will not stop talking.

"He didn't write them. He had to ask another man to write his letters because he couldn't. And when he got letters from us, he had to ask someone else to read them." She looks at us, then says in her hurried way, "He could sign his name." Her voice is so soft that both my brothers look down at the Melmac plates as though there are bugs in the food.

Shoving around some mashed potatoes, Toms asks, "Why couldn't he?"

My father answers for her. "He never went to school."

"Not ever?" This from Rick, the quieter one. I know why he is surprised. We thought everyone went to school. All the adults in our lives have gone to school unless there was a problem like my aunt's polio, which left something wrong with her. Some, like Mom and Dad, didn't finish high school because they were needed on the farms. Still, all the other adults we knew of learned to read and write. Of this I am sure. When they talk about reading and writing, they talk about it as if it has something to do with church, that holy.

"He was the youngest of a dozen." My mother pauses, gathering memories as she would berries in a patch. "His mother died when he was born. He came to this country when he was twelve. He learned to farm, but it was hard. He had to ask about things . . ." She stops again. I can feel it, a snag in her voice, catches of the unfinished story, things covered up. I remember Grandpa Joe smoking his Camels in the living room, listening to the game shows on the radio. I take a breath, about to ask. She stops it. "That's what happens if you don't get an education." I roll it around in my mouth. It is a big word, a new word. *Education.*

This word is all about reading. I want to read with all my heart because I want to know the end of the stories in the fancy books, the ones my mother calls fairy tales, though there are not a lot of fairies in them. There are not many books in our house, and they tend to have frayed pages or pencil lines where my siblings have scribbled. But of the books we have, there are two I carry to her night after night. They have hard covers with raised pictures on them. One is called *Grimm's* and the other *Andersen's*. The stories in these books are so long that I fall asleep before they are done, but the words are big and fill my mouth like peaches. Words like *stallion* for a boy horse that *gallops* and *magic* for something that you make happen by *casting a spell,* though my mother isn't sure if she should read these to me. Some of them are scary, but I like the way they make me tingle. The pictures they make in my mind stay there, like the image of the little match girl who dies on the street. Or the snow queen in her dark sleigh. And there is also the Bible with its black cover and gold letters and, inside, a million small letters and numbers, and when she reads these stories, I learn all the old names: Moses, Abraham, Noah. Even my mother's name is there, Ruth.

My mother doesn't have time to read aloud anymore, or if she does she chooses stories for my sisters and brothers that are shorter and have more pictures. They come and go in the house like leaves blowing through open doors. When I ask her where she gets them, she tells me from a place called the *liberry*. She says she read the big books to me because they were *what we had*. She tells me they were gifts from "a long time ago, before you kids." I sit on the edge of her bed as she reads the short stories, but my mind drifts. When she carries the little girls to bed, I hold the book as she has, open as a day, and I tell myself the stories of battles and beheadings. I turn pages and make up voices. When I come to the blank pages at the end, my hands always turn cold because there is something else going on, but I do not have words for it. It has to do with a whisper about our babysitter, that she *wasn't smart enough to read*. Or when a cousin said of a hired hand, "That guy is so dumb he can't read."

Understanding swims toward me with its nuzzling awareness. It's not just that people should want to read so they have this *education,* but if they can't read they are dumb. I know what dumb is. People who are dumb can't speak; they have no words at all—like the blank pages. This is the reason my mother's voice dives under the covers when she speaks of my grandfather.

Warming up on the heat register in the Oomen farmhouse

The Kelly School shapes the days of farm kids from all over the township. In that boxy room with unfiltered light, dog-eared books, we settle into this thing called education. I learn I am in a grade, *kinnygarten*. I am one of two in this grade. Gus, the other, always has a runny nose but he is older, seven, and his freckles and almost red hair seem warm to me. I sit in front of him in the smaller seats. I know he likes me because he brings me a soft stone that marks on concrete so I can draw hopscotch lines at lunch.

One day, as I sit in the dull light, the teacher gives me a practice book. Some of the pages have been worked by another boy who came to school for a few days but then didn't come back because *he had problems.*

"You can finish his book," she says, opening to the page where I should begin. She bends over my desk, breathing like it is a lot of work. She points to a row of ducks. One duck is set apart. Then four more ducks. She says, "Find the duck that matches." I don't see how they are different. She shows me what the other boy did, how he chose wrong. I stare at his circle, a small ghost, his lines like fine twigs. I look at the pictures, five ducks in a row. Following her finger, I see one duck has a crooked wing, one is without a foot, so they are not a match. I touch my pencil to the page where one duck has all its parts. My lines are heavy, my circle around the duck slow and clumsy. What if I make the same mistake the boy did? I scuff my feet against the floor.

We do this same lesson with cows, pigs, and finally lambs. We have never had lambs on our farm so I do not know what is right for them. From there, she asks me to match numbers and letters. She asks me to make letters of my name. I learn four letters, a *simple way* she tells me because two are alike, which *should be easy.* My lines are crooked, tilted like there is bad weather on the page. More scuffing until I am scolded for making too much noise.

One day the teacher announces, "Now we are going to learn to read."

At last. I wiggle in my desk. I know books hold the answers to the *why* questions. My fingertips quiver when I trace the letters on the fancy covers. I want this.

I am placed with kids who are all second and third graders because the teacher doesn't have time to develop lessons for just the two youngest, me and Gus, and so *let's put them with the others and they will catch on.* But I don't catch on.

Every day I leave my seat and walk to the half-circle of small chairs at the front. I face the blackboard with its puzzling clouds, a place where words have been but now are erased. We take turns reading and the teacher says, "Yes, yes." When it comes my turn, I start to say the words they have said, looking down as I have seen them do, and when I look up she says "No, no, that's not what is says." She says, "Read the words, child." I look at the words and start again, but she says "No, no, not words you make up, the words on the page. The letters make a word." I stop. What does she mean? I look at the chalkboard where the big letters march across the top like prancing ponies. That's the alphabet, these are words. What's the trick?

We are sent back to our seats. She calls the older kids to numbers. I walk slowly, staring down at the sand that pools under each desk like a tiny hill. I sit, scuffing. My head feels like I hit it on something hard. I fold my arms and put my head down on my desk but leave a little dark place to peak sideways under my arms at the other kids who have books open. *They read. Why can't I?*

Every day I return to the half-circle at the front of the one room. I keep trying but instead of the voices of other readers, I hear the desks sawing against the dirty floor. The coal furnace ticks its secrets in the corner. Each time I am called on, I say the words I hear the others say, but they are never right. I realize I am making a guess, always wrong.

Gus learns to read. I cannot believe it. When she calls on him, he speaks slowly and his face scrunches up so I know it is hard, but he fingers out one word after another. *See. Run. Look.* Little words that don't do much. Not *gallop.* Not *magic.* Words that are fun to say. He learns to read the names of the boy and girl in his book. *Dick. Jane.* He can look at the word and know. I wonder why I have never met anyone named Dick or Jane, no one among all the people on all the farms is named Dick or Jane. I wonder why no one in the book is named Katherine or Evelyn or Henry, or even Noah, a name I know from the Bible stories. But Gus knows Dick and Jane. It is the first time I am drawn to someone for what they have that I don't have. I look at him and smile.

Gus becomes my friend. He sits next to me during the lesson and he points to words as the other kids say them. He tells me when there is a new word. His grubby finger moves along my book when the other kids read. The new words are all little, not big, not the ones I like to say even when they are hard. But none of that matters because I cannot read even the little words. As we learn more little words, I forget the big words. I forget *magic*. I say only the little words Gus whispers to me.

One day, Gus and I are saying the little words back and forth like tiny drumbeats in the air between us. Suddenly the teacher looks right at me over the big book where she follows along. She uses her sharp-as-broken-glass voice, "*You* have to do your own work." She makes a decision, "Gus, why don't you sit here?" It is not a real why question. She points to a faraway chair where a third grader who stole second base sits. He is to trade with Gus. Gus stands and walks slowly to the other end of the circle. He sits in the third grader's chair. The third grader looks mad. He plops in the smaller chair next to me and will not look at me. The little drum fades. Gus seems far away. It must be as far to his chair as it is to walk home.

Now the paper crackles like winter when I turn the pages. When I repeat the words, they are like a toy train with all the hitches broken. Nothing stays together. The teacher knows. She scolds. We try again. The next time, when I look at her, she is looking at another boy in the second row, a fourth grader who just wet his pants again. I look down, thinking *now*. While she is busy with this boy who the whole room is tittering about—*Read.* So that when she comes back she will not look at me with a red face. So no one will think I am not smart enough for school. But the letters are not like the words when I say them out loud. They sit on the page like tiny insects. When my teacher comes back from taking care of the boy who wet his pants, she skips me, moves on to the next child, a second grader who knows even more words than Gus.

After that, when her voice snakes out into the classroom, calling for reading lesson, I always have to pee. I have to leave the gray warmth of the room. I raise my hand and walk to the back of the classroom where all the hooks are weighted down with rough wools and the floor is cluttered with muck-scented buckle boots now that it is winter. I find my coat next to Gus's, shoulder into it, and waddle to the outhouse. At first the teacher sends an older girl with me, especially when it's cold. She says to the girl, "Now Theresa, see little Anne does her business."

When the teacher figures out that I am trying to escape the reading lesson, she stops sending someone else with me. I have to go alone if I am to go at all. I walk down the icy steps and along the path to the outhouse behind the old school. I trudge out into the thin snow, to the closetlike structure that sits on the edge of my own father's field. I pull open the wooden door. The rusted metal spring squeaks like a mouse not yet dead from the cats. I sit on the cold seat and stare in the dim light at the uninsulated walls, at the two by fours where the big boys have carved words into the walls. Just this year all the words have been painted over because some are bad words. The big girl told me this. *Bad Words.* The paint makes the wood look like the blank pages. But if the word was carved with a good enough knife, the lines—like in the workbook I used—show through like ghosts. In the darkened, smelly space I reach out and trace them with my fingertips. These words are like the words in the reading book. Each one seems to have the same number of letters as the words in the book. Little words, but bad, the big girl said. *We must never say them.* These must be the words I have heard in the yard, on the baseball field. These are part of the big world. The big boys say them and get told to *watch it.* They have to wash out their mouths because of these words. These words have such a big sound built right in them that no one says them softly. They are like the dynamite my father set off. Little words with big sounds that leave a hole in your mouth. No one should say them. My mother would tell me not to say them. But she is not here. Does she know I want to say them, even though I am as little as these words? I want the big sound to come out of my mouth with that hardness like when you hit someone. I want the big hard words. I trace the letters of the words that I cannot speak but I think I know. I can almost read them. But I cannot speak them unless I can read them. I look at the blank wall with its ghost words that are the real words that I want. I sit in the dark and trace the words and let the feeling of being dumb wash over me until I am too cold to move and it is recess and I have to call for someone to help me.

SAVED

May is a rough collection of cool days and lilacs, of planting beans and changing my littlest sister's diapers. My mother and father are *hard at it,* as Grandpa Henry calls it, which means they are working in the fields and barns and always looking at the weather. The winter has been filled with unexpected things: a baby who would have been a new cousin died when it was born; and my Grandpa Joe, my mother's father, died of something called a stroke. We all went to the funeral. There was a casket again and people with wet faces making sounds like an animal held too long and struggling to get away. Where they buried my grandpa, old soldiers shot their guns, together, over and over because he fought in the same war they did, though I don't understand how the gunshots all together make honor.

And there is still the problem: I cannot read.

Gus walks home with me, up the gravel road with its weedy ditches and gray ruts to the end of our driveway. Although he has even more siblings than I do, he sometimes stays. If no one has chores for us or if no

littler person needs watching, we sit under the crab apple tree and he tells
me stories of what he sees on their TV. Sometimes he brings comics and
reads them to me.

One day he tells me about Superman. These are not fairy stories
like the ones my mother has read to me. This story is about a man who
can fly, a man so strong he can save people from dying, even from being hurt. He can do this because he is not from here but from a planet,
a place in the sky. The stories stick in my brain like the burrs that knot
my hair in the weed patch. I touch the stories, pulling on them when I
am alone, thinking that maybe Superman could save a person from the
dynamite, from the sound and the hole, or from the cellar, or from the
dreams that come to me at night so clear I cannot move but in the morning I cannot remember them either.

Today we are walking home together. I look at the dust rising from
my dirty shoes and I ask the question I have come to. "Gus, will you save
me?" He looks up from the stone he is hiding in an empty chew box. He
stares at its round shape admiringly before he pops the lid in place. He
stuffs the container in his pocket. "From what?"

"Stuff."

"Sure," he says, glancing around for the threat. "How?"

"Play Superman with me." His freckles disappear as the color comes
up in his face. He nods slowly and reaches his arms out in front of him
the way they show Superman in the comics. I nod back at him. "You
could fly," I say. When we get to my house, I steal our one blue towel for
his cape and show him how to run with it flapping behind him, just like
he was flying.

I tell him how it must go, like in the comics. "I pretend to be in
danger. And you pretend to fly, and you come save me."

"But you're not in danger."

"Yes, I am," I tell him, confused that he doesn't see. But he is my
friend, and so we climb trees and I tell him to leap down to save me from
the brown monster (though he tells me three times it is just our beagle).
But still, I say, and over time he understands that I see something different from what he does and he just has to do as I ask, which is daring and

scary and makes him feel sweaty and good. I can tell because sometimes he just laughs.

We become two shadows of a story that is always happening and I love him for this, that every chance we get, *he saves me.* So we hide in the barns and he jumps between the bays and saves me from the bull, or from the giant pigeons that live in the silo, though my father stops that adventure cold because he doesn't want anyone playing where the silage falls. And when Gus leaves me to walk the long mile to his small house on the dirt two-track, we feel sad to leave each other, like something is gone from the day once we cannot be who we never really are but who we want to be.

My skin feels different when I am saved.

I believe, as a child can believe, that he is Superman and that he will save me—and then I will be safe from . . . what? The sounds of guns in a cemetery, the letters that will not tell me their secrets? The mouth cannot say the right thing.

Behind the farmhouse in the backyard, near the clotheslines but opposite the crab apple tree, a small chicken coop, red and square, sits in the middle of a grassy yard. This spring has been so cold we do not have chickens. My mother has shoveled out the manure for the garden and used the push broom to clear the floor. Three casement windows set with small panes of glass make it so the baby chicks will have light when we have them again. An eye hook latches on the outside so the dogs can't get in. We are there, playing Superman, when I ask Gus to lock me inside the chicken coop. He does so. He stands in the ankle-length grass, the blue towel tied around his shoulders, and he stares hard at the door, seeing through it.

"Save me, Gus," I call out the window, picking the old caulk off the mulleins as I do.

His red hair is alive in the May light, and he steps back, lifts his hands to the clothesline and hangs on the taut cord for a minute, working up his rescue. My mother would yell at him for this. I am just about to tell him so when he throws his shoulders back, roars a boy roar, runs and leaps toward the door, his blue cape flopping. I know what he must do. He must burst through the locked door and fracture it into a hundred pieces. I watch him lope across the grass and I know nothing will stop him; he will blast through and I will see the big light where the door had been and I will be saved. But he does not touch it. He stops short with a confused mutter, meandering back to the clothesline. He looks at his feet for a while; then, just as I am about to tell him again what to do, he runs at the door. But again he stops short with a grunt, something about its solidness stopping him. I don't understand. I stand inside, waiting to see what will happen when the wood explodes like dynamite. But nothing happens.

It dawns on me that we must be doing something wrong. Since the door is locked, I push the rotting window casement open and climb out on a wobbly frame, making a new plan as I do. I will be the one to hang on to the clothesline, because that looked like fun and it's against the rules. I won't be able to let go, because it is really a *spider's web,* didn't we always know that? Like in the fairy tales, it's sticky and it won't let me go. I tell him, "You go in. You be in the chicken house, and I'm trapped in this web and you break out to save me." For a moment we both hang on the clothesline, swaying and looking at each other.

"Time to save me, Gus," I say. He stares up at his hands and looks confused by the insistence of his small friend, who is too worried about this one thing when he is just enjoying hanging from the clothesline. But for all of his plain being, he is my friend, and if I want to be saved, well, he must find a way. He walks to the door, unlocks it, steps into the shadow, and turns toward me.

"Lock it," he says and pulls the door closed. I let go of the line and run to lock the door, thrilled. I hurry back to the clothesline, reach up, and grab the line, dragging it down. I hang on as if I can't let go, my feet scrabbling in the grass. I call to him in a voice that I hope is like Lois Lane's. "Oh, no, I'm trapped, Gus. Save me." I watch the door. The world slows down, takes on light.

But Gus has figured something out, something that was bothering him all along. Gus thinks maybe a person cannot break through a locked wooden door. He thinks there must be another way to do this.

Although I do not know it yet, glass is beautiful in its breaking.

He paces back and forth in the chicken house, waving his arms and talking to himself. He backs into a shadowy corner, paces first one way and then the other, swinging his arms, stopping once to reach for the ceiling. Then he turns and lowers his arms into the flying position. The small body shifts, moves into sudden blue motion as the boy shape hurdles forward, not toward the solid boards of the door but directly toward the light, toward the eight frail panels of thin and dirty glass. Gus, my Superman, lifts his short legs and churns forward. He roars, pushes off with his grimy feet, and leaps. Momentum lifts and carries his body in a short arc. For a breathtaking moment, he is covered with light, flying toward me, the flash of blue towel rising like the entire sky. And then the impact, the clear territory of surprise and shock rising into the air all around us as the small panes and old mulleins break into stars, suns, a thousand pieces of light and color all erupting out from the white face and blue towel.

I gasp. This is what saving is: all the bright things of the world spinning into shards, a shattering of something you can't see but is there. The force of his small body, lightning on bright water.

And then his voice rises like rope pulled too tight, a high twine of sound all wrong, caught and strained in a sharpness that cuts. Cold runs through my own small frame. I let go of the clothesline and run, screaming that Gus jumped through the window and *Mama come, come save us.*

Her hands wet from laundry, she hurries out of the house onto the porch, into the sunlight of the backyard. Her eyes fray with fear and irritation, but in the time it takes to breathe, she takes it all in. She grabs the small boy by his blue cape and, with the quick efficiency of an old nurse, tells him to stop crying right now. He looks back at her, his mouth gaping, but he swallows snot and tears and something that has made his skin white again. Then she lifts and examines and sops up blood, marking in her mind every cut and scrape as she marks it on his body with iodine.

She pulls two tiny sparkling shards out of his knuckles while he bites his lips. She exhausts our precious supply of Band-Aids, but she is breathing more easily. Although she holds him there in the grass for a long time, when she begins to scold, I know he will be all right. His eyes clear up and he climbs off her lap. In silence she picks up the glass and rakes the grass; she shakes her head and scolds again, more shrilly. He says nothing, looking down at his feet. He drops the blue towel and stands aside.

Finally she asks, "What on earth were you doing?"

He is silent.

"We were playing Superman." I chirp this with a kind of confidence that will become my trademark in difficult situations. My mother takes a long look at me and says softly, in a whisper that makes this name mean something different from what I thought it would mean— "*Superman?*"—slowly, like chewing something sour.

She sends Gus home, saying that she will call his mother. I watch him, bandaged, shuffling slowly down the driveway. He does not look back. Then she turns to me and speaks so softly I almost can't hear. "He could have died. He could have cut himself so badly he could have died."

I cannot tell her that he was supposed to save me. That he did not save me.

Windows break, light scatters.

He could never save me.

I know that some things can never be taken back: some words, death, the body through air. I know a body can bleed and hurt and still be saved. Gus is saved. Hurt but saved. Gus has made a moment that I will turn to again and again in my small memory, his body hurtling through the broken light. Glass is beautiful when it breaks. But the glass is still broken. Something is beautiful but broken when a person is saved. I am not saved, was never saved from anything, not from pigeons or bulls or the sound of dynamite or guns in a cemetery or dreams in the night.

I feel two things at once: the glass and the window without its glass, all blown. My mother leaves me standing in the grass.

I go back to school but I do not talk to Gus. It is the cruelest thing a little girl can do, isn't it? To sit in the wood and iron desk with Gus behind me and never turn around again. After that we are always awkward with each other, scuffing dirt and not speaking. I begin to dread school, for there is always something unspoken, something broken I must learn that has nothing to do with words.

Picnic

The tiger lilies thicken with orange bloom all along the bank in front of Kelly School, where I have just finished *kindergarten,* a word I can almost say, though I cannot spell or read it. Most words are secrets. I already believe this as I walk toward this school that has made me feel like the knot at the center of the rope in tug of war, pulled first one way, then another. Hard lessons and warm sweaters. Shabby books and funny songs. Warm light from old windows and dry mud that clumps under the desks in the exact shape of boot treads. Fifteen children making a story out of a year. But for me it has not been a good story.

I ask my mother, "Why are you having a picnic?"

"It's the end of the school year." There is a story in her voice but she does not tell it.

Today the lilies lie sideways, their slim green stems resting one on top of the other in layers because just that morning a thunderstorm rolled through the county and hard rain knocked down the flowers. When we turn into the yard, Tom and Rick trailing like kite tails, I am surprised

40

to see the men there. Is it because of this rain? Now that they know the corn will come along fine, they can take this moment to linger and be fed. They lean against the fence or stand, arms crossed, boots set apart. They smoke or chew. The air has a sharpness that comes only at this time of year, a light so short and bright it cuts.

The picnic has already begun when my mother and I carry the baskets past the lilies and into the school yard. Card tables have been unfolded and set, spindly legs braced with stones, to hold trays of sand-wiches and potato salad. Hot dishes with flowered towels over them keep noodles warm even though it is already warm enough to sweat. Big boys play baseball. They shout *batter, batter, batter,* as though these words are meant for the whole world, not just this half-yard, half-field dotted with the flat rocks they use for bases.

The grown-ups, gathered here and there to watch, laugh the kind of laughter they make when they can't figure out how to say what's on their minds. I don't know why. Only sometimes, I see a grandpa shake his head or a neighbor look up at the bell and blow his nose. Once, I fol-low a man into the big room, now empty of children. He stoops, touches the backs of the smallest chairs where we sit for lessons. He stares a long time at the cloudy blackboard. When he turns, his face cannot solve the puzzle.

In the yard, my mother greets other mothers with her friendly phone voice. She asks after their moms and dads. She wants to know how the winter was for them and if things are going all right. She moves among them. Her voice, the rise and fall of it as she enters into talk with Mrs. Smith, or Raymond Jenson, or Evelyn or Dolores, is like ties in patchwork, pulling the layers together.

I sit on the stoop and watch my first school picnic. It is like Sunday dinner, I think, but outside. These people are coming back to their old school to talk about it so it stays in place. They all went here. They have to come back, like my cousins on the Fourth of July. The eighth grad-ers, four of them, are dressed up a little. The boy who wet his pants in February is drinking Coke from a small bottle and laughing at the fat

man who is umpire, the one who calls *safe* with a voice that sounds as
though it comes from inside a silo. The girl whose tooth got knocked out
by someone in her own family smiles for the first time. Gus takes a turn
at bat, though he is too short, but then he hits the ball straight past the
shortstop and everyone claps. My brothers and some other boys drag in
a bucket of frogs they've caught in the ditch. My baby sister toddles on a
blanket. On the table, someone sets a cracked jar of spring leeks, which
the men cut and eat like apples.

The talk flutters, stops here and there like a bird hunting for worms,
but never settles. Then, as if they hear the same call, the women move
together to lift wax paper and towels off bowls, speaking all the while
of the price of milk, the yard goods sale at Gambles, how many inches
of rain that storm dumped, and if anything got struck by lightning. The
noise and drift of games fades, replaced by the small, sharp sounds of
cutlery against stoneware, like insects banging a tin light. The men line
up to fill their plates. They sprawl like broken toys, complaining of their
backs, in the grass or on old quilts. They balance the plates on their knees
and look out at the warm air and clear light. They settle close enough to
one another to be called friendly. They make a moment that they will not
remember because what they will remember happened before.

I know this because they start to tell the stories.

They tell stories about one older boy who hooked a tractor to the
school's outhouse and pulled it over before he realized the teacher was
in there. They point to Harold and laugh and repeat, gasping, *Old guy
never knew what hit him.* They tell the story of Old Clay luring a cow to
the top of the woodshed and then removing the chute. The joke turned
backward because Old Clay had to climb up there every day to feed and
milk her. A tall, skinny man lifts his finger and tells how, climbing down
the ladder, he spilled a whole pail of milk onto an eighth-grade girl who
was all dressed up to go to a wedding. A woman turns bright red and they
laugh, covering their bad teeth and holding their sides. Their voices pick
up and pull together like stitching, telling how the cow lived up there for
a week before someone, maybe it was Jack, he was smart like that, figured out how to get her down. They tell about Emmet, who scrambled

to the top of the school and stole the bell's clapper so it wouldn't ring. They tell about the boy who could fart at will—but didn't he almost drown in the pond playing hooky, crawl out covered with green muck and stinking even more? They laugh like people who weren't supposed to laugh in church, and then can. They laugh until they have to take off their caps and wipe their foreheads and say, "Whoo-whee, that's a good one."

They look at one another and say names that come from when the stories were tricks and not yet stories. The stories are told *on* someone, not *about* someone. It is like tattling, but this tattling makes their faces look like water fresh from the well. When it is just quiet and the plates are sopped clean with soft bread and the last soda has been tipped up, an old man shoots pop out of his nose in a foamy stream. They laugh so hard they have to bend over, and tears come out of their eyes they are so happy that he can still do it after all this time.

After that, they cannot look at one another. It is like the part of a church song that gets quieter. They stare down at the grass that has been bent into a rough mat by their scuffing. They stare at the sky, so blue it hurts their eyes. The women collect plates and move the bucket of frogs over to the ditch where Mr. Ray will pour them out when Tom and Rick and the other little boys aren't looking. Some grandmas play cards on a blanket. Marijo cries, needing a nap. Mr. Carter turns on a car radio and reports the Tigers' score. I listen to the low half-murmur of people who have known one another all their lives, whose words shift and flow around the clot of bologna sandwich they are chewing, but still they understand the words.

A cluster of women gathers at the bottom of the stoop, where they can keep an eye on the last of the food and the little boys. At first, their voices are like bright water, but then one pulled, tight voice says, "So, the last one. After fifty years."

My mother's silence makes me listen more closely.

"Do you think we'll miss this old place? I thought we did okay here, you know? I thought it was good," Mrs. Smith says.

A young mother whose hair is not yet gray says, "But our kids should have a place to wash their hands after they take a leak, don't you think?" And for some reason this tickles them.

"I'll miss the bell," one says.

My mother speaks. "It'll still be here. It just won't be a school."

"It'll be closed."

And the oldest says, "We won't come back here." The quiet drifts into the shadows of the trees. They move to clean up.

But I have heard it. The school is closing, not just for summer but for always. They are saying a good-bye. So that is why the men are here. I watch them go about what makes a picnic, but now I know why this is not like other picnics where I have eaten the warm potato salad and played the game where you tie one of your own legs to someone else's and try to run. Everyone is fine, yes, but they are like the cloudy water in the pond. They have had enough endings, because just this winter Aunt Minnie's baby died, and sometimes things get so lost they can't be found and if they don't come here, will everyone forget the stories?

I cannot tell them.

I cannot say out loud that I want to run around in circles and shout the one thing I know for sure. I will not have to come back here. Not come back. So as the afternoon moves through its rituals that are like a party and like going to church too, I hold the thing inside, that I am so glad this thing is done: this little year, this *kindergarten*. For those hours at the picnic, I believe I will never again have to sit and look at letters and pretend to know something I do not know.

I wander the yard. I look at the lilies with their trumpets tipped to the ground. I wonder if, when the water is all gone from their leaves, they will stand up again or just lie down like this until the orange tongues of their petals shrivel and drop off. Someone goes into the school and rings the bell, and everyone looks up, listening to its long words. They are standing apart now, each a little alone. They will not come back together like this. I go back into the picnic like the little girl I am, slipping in among people like a fish in water. I will remember this, I think. I will remember the lilies leaning down in the shade and what I learned on this day. When I have the way to understand, I will say the bell's words held all my happiness, all their sorrow, and my first secret.

Kindergarten school photo

The Ledger

At the end of the picnic, Kelly School's nicked door, the one with so many handprints around the knob that it has turned charcoal colored, is locked with a heavy iron key. No one goes there now.

The grown-ups talk a lot, late at night after cards, or over coffee as they lean on the running boards of their trucks. Their voices are two ways, sorting something out. They talk about where their kids will go. For the news is that the townships will close all one-room schoolhouses. They will build a new school, a community school, with six or seven or eight new classrooms under one roof, and each grade will be in a separate room.

I giggle when I think about the new school because I am happy that I will not return to the old one.

But the men shake their heads because taxes will *skyrocket* and the money from the government is not enough. So there is to be something called a public sale with sealed bids and numbers. Kelly School has to be sold before other work can begin. One day my father stands in the kitchen with a white envelope poking up from the pocket of his work shirt like a little flag. In the envelope is the number he and my mother have agreed upon. He will go to a meeting all about the white envelope. He puts his coffee down and looks at her, and they both sigh and smile sour little smiles like berries that aren't quite sweet.

And then something so unusual that my mother hurries to explain it every time someone asks. My father's bid is accepted. He has bought the schoolhouse, contents, and land for the phenomenal price of three hundred dollars. In a household where every penny is counted, where even shoes are repaired and handed down, the number is like the stars.

I ask him, "How much is three hundred dollars? Is it a million?"

"It's what two acres is worth." He does not want to talk about this number.

But my mother looks at him and says, "Tell her."

He stares out the kitchen window at the fields. He rubs his chin and says, "It's what education costs." And my mother makes one quick nod to me.

"The townships will have to consolidate now," she says.

What a word. *Consolidate.* I ask my mother what it means. She searches her mind for a minute before she decides what to say, "It means coming together."

I cannot say *consolidate,* but I think the word smells like oranges.

My father is doing it so the new school can happen. But also, my father owns the two acres of land and the schoolhouse.

I am free of it and not free of it.

Days after the picnic, we pack into the truck and drive the few hundred yards to the school. Uncle Joe, who is curious about what can be salvaged, has joined us. He tells jokes in which one word means two things, so we laugh a lot when he is around. We all climb the stoop except my littlest sister; my mom leaves her to nap in a basket on the grass where she can hear her cry. My father uses the big key to unlock the door of the one-room school, and we stand for a moment looking at the room, which seems as dim as a cellar, before we step into the dusty light. The desks look filthy—their carvings grim with dirt; the piano is as dark as a bear, the blackboard pocked, the floors stained with soot. We walk around the room, quieted by how old it has become already, how hollow, as though it has already been empty a long time.

Tom and Rick abandon us for the frogs, but my mother walks around, touches things, turns over chairs to look at the supports, peers inside the desks. Some have parts missing; one no longer has a seat. She pauses over the books, most without covers, fanning the pages. She looks at my uncle. "They let this place go to pot, didn't they?"

"More ways than one," he says with a snicker. I giggle.

"Didn't have money to keep it up," my father says as he moves in and out of the mudroom. I wish he would stop, but both he and my mother set to it, their hands making the disorder that comes before order. She wants to find out what she can sell to make up for the price that has been paid. She has paper in her shirt pocket. She will make lists. She is thinking the way she does when she buys fabric to make a dress. She counts and separates the old desks because there is some interest in *Early American things.* She shoves the good ones to the side. She says the world is changing and that some people will want old things to help them re-member.

I don't want to remember. I want the new school. I want this place to stay closed. "Why can't you just leave this stuff here?"

My father is already moving the broken desks out onto the flatbed to take to the burn pile. "Because someone's gonna live here." He pulls down a green shade and lets go. It flaps wildly, like a trapped bird.

"*Live here?*" I look to my mother.

"We're going to change this into a house for a Mexican family coming from Texas." She is sorting the books. "They'll help us in the asparagus fields." She sees my face. "We can't keep up anymore."

She opens an old cabinet, pulls out dozens of green ledgers, and drops them into a pile of old newspapers. The dust puffs out from where they land on the floor. Uncle Joe works on the big coal stove, figuring out how it is put together. The door squeaks as he yanks it open. The world seems full of so many new things that I cannot keep them straight. I wander around this room, which is the color of a dirty palm. My father will make Kelly School into a house for strangers from the place called Texas. I will go to a new school. There is a story being made. I feel as happy as chickens in the morning.

I kneel on the floor next to the pile of ledgers and open one. Names run all down one side in columns, and in another column letters line up in a little march. I recognize the alphabet and I know these must be kids' names. I can match the common ones with names on the mailboxes down the road, but I cannot read them. I do know what As and Bs and Cs are and I know what they mean. They are our marks. The marks are little secrets about how we did. I do not know my marks, only that I *passed,* that I can *go on.*

My mother enters from the back room, wiping her hands on a rag and complaining that the remaining food from the picnic was left in some boxes and is spoiled. She lifts a piece of white bread to show me green bologna. I show her the ledgers, struggling to open the bulky canvas covers. My father passes by, carrying wooden chairs that are so broken they will be burned. She glances at him. "John, look. The old grade books." He is breathing hard because the chairs are heavy and he wants this room cleared so he can begin making a house. "Should we save them?" she asks.

"I dunno," he has his busy voice.

Uncle Joe walks over, glances at the pages. His eyes twinkle. He recognizes a name. "We could have some fun with this."

That decides it for my mother. He loves a prank, but she is different.

"It's not our business." She turns back to the cabinets.

I am surprised by this. I ask, "How come?" I like the ledgers, the green feel of fabric covers. I like their many-ness, their repeated squares all across a page, the big sheets. Some are blank. I could pretend to write in them.

"We might hurt someone's feelings. We'll respect their privacy."

"What about their privates?" My mother shoots him a look, then grins. My uncle snorts and turns back to the stove. My father makes big noise hauling more chairs.

I know about privacy, because it is what one has in the bathroom. And someday, when I need more privacy, my mother has said I will have a room of my own. But I do not understand why we need privacy for our marks. I want to know who got what mark and, more important, what I got. My mother takes the grade books from my hands and closes them and puts them firmly in the crate of things to be burned. But when she returns to the back of the room, I reach into the box. I find a ledger like my teacher used. I open one, run my fingers down the columns, looking for my name. I can recognize my name, but every time I find an Oomen name, it has a different start-up name. I flip the green pages, running my stubby fingers down the columns, turning more pages, looking at the marks.

Uncle Joe squats and looks over my shoulder. "I am not here," I say.

He reaches his big hands down to flip the pages. They sound like old leaves brushing against each other. I hold the book to him and I lean a little into him, hoping he will put his arm around me the way my dad would. He does not. He turns more pages, looks again, finally grins. "Guess you didn't go to school after all." He chuckles, winks, and moves back to the furnace. "Maybe you'll have to start over." He calls over his shoulder with his big-joke smile.

This makes me feel like broken glass inside. Here in the light falling through dirty windows is a place where I was but now I am not. I have been lost or erased, and all that I learned, the naming of animals and the counting of small and large things, feels as though it is gone.

My mother enters, scribbling on her paper. She hears me say to my uncle, "I don't care. I'm going to the castle-aded school. I'll never go to a school like this again." She knows I mean *consolidated,* but she's hearing something else for the first time. She's hearing a mistake. I can see it in her face. She is about to correct something, to make something right. I hate it already.

"It will be a while before you go to the consolidated school."

I look at her for so long I feel the light change. "I'm going. You said."

"The school won't be finished for a year, maybe two."

This sinks in slowly.

"You said I won't go here."

"You won't. You'll go to Cleveland School."

"Cleveland?"

"You know where that is."

But I can't think where it is. I can't think at all. I am not going to the school where they will teach me to read? Where they will for sure have my name in the place where I can find it?

"I'm not going to the new school?"

She answers the real question. "Not enough kids were coming back here, so they put Kelly School kids with the Cleveland School kids. There will be enough to keep that school open for a year."

Uncle Joe pulls his hands, blackened with soot, out of some inner part of the furnace. "It's down the road from my place. East of the big hill."

I don't know what east is, but I know the big hill where my dad can find mushrooms in the spring.

"I'll show you next time we go to town," she says, turning to stack and lift old sheet music from the piano.

But on its own, Cleveland School surfaces in my head. I do know it. It is on the way to Crystal Valley. It has a bigger field for baseball. It has bathrooms at the back that are connected to the building. It is like Kelly School but bigger. I have seen it many times, but it has never been connected to me. I turn a page in the ledger without looking at it. Another. I keep turning, faster and faster, until I am nearly tearing the pages. My mother puts down the sheet music she is carrying to the truck, places her hand on my shoulder, and says softly that I *should help now.* I close the book with a slap. I carry the grade books out. One by one, I throw them in the big red-brown barrel and watch the flames wash over them.

But at the last minute, I pull one from the pile. My mother sees me do it, sighs but lets it go. She tells me, "That one is old, from the thirties.

You can play with it for now."

"Names are in it," I say, thinking of the privacy word.

"No one you know."

But their marks are still there. I look at the marks following the names, the way they fill the little squares. I know that the person who had that name did something in this school a long time ago. The marks tell a story so important they have to be kept.

After that, the door to the school is always unlocked so that my father can go there whenever he has the time to work on it. I go there alone. I play school. I list marks on the board with pieces of abandoned chalk. I try to unlock the secret of the grade book, the private moment made public in which one finds one's own name recorded and the mark tells how you did. I make up names for the people in the book I saved, and I write pretend grades in every blank square. I look out the windows at the freshly tilled soil where the new asparagus field will be. The windows in every direction are full of fields named for the crop they grow. Even fields have names. Schools have names. People have names and we say them. We write them down.

But I am not there. I look for the first time at my own invisibility. It rests in those pages, the possibility that no one will see me; no one will ever know how I did. I wonder if I am not important enough to be on a list that includes everyone else in my world.

What I Know

What saves me now: I am sitting on the porch steps with my father. The old farmhouse looms behind us, peeling and alive with its feverish cry for order. But we are on the porch after supper, staring through the branches of the silver maple across the yard and down the road to the west. It is near sunset. That time of evening when everything turns golden. He has come out to drink a beer, to cool off. He is waiting for my mother. He knows he should send me in to help her, but he doesn't. He knows it is my turn to dry the dishes. I look at him; he looks at me and sips. He does not speak. We both know this moment is like finding an arrowhead in the fields. We cannot bear to give it away.

Around us the stone pillars of the porch rise in their tattered splendor. Here and there, a rock has fallen from its mortared niche, and what is left is like the inside of a bird's egg. I like to set smaller stones into these hollows, green or blue stones that are hard to find. I look at it, a small green stone in a place where a bigger gray stone had been. Like a cradle or nest. As though this small stone could grow to fit the place that had been left by something larger.

Between the two wings of the railing that surrounds the porch, concrete steps spill out onto the irregular wreck of a yard. The steps are cracked with weather and years, as are the railings, which were designed as sitting places. But these benchlike shapes hold the cold, even in summer. When I straddle them and whine that the cold is *coming into me like knives*—a phrase I have heard my mother use—he reaches up for me. I climb onto his lap. I curl in his arms.

I am being held by my father.

The light comes through the trees and dapples our skin. I touch his buttons, his duck-billed farm cap, the tiny top-spiral notebook he keeps in his shirt pocket. I pull on the dark curly hair that scrambles from his open collar. His skin smells of soil and soap and sweat, his hands of manure, fuel, dirt, and tires. His breath is tobacco and coffee. If I had grown-up words, I would say his is the scent of industry and earth.

Although I can speak perfectly, I whisper to him. I giggle for him. And though he is still, doesn't even look at me, I know that he holds me in his arms with the same wonder he holds new seeds, in the unadorned and practical awe that I am his little girl. I have seen this in his face and already I know it deeply. This knowledge makes the hollow places I live in less cold, the noisy places less loud. The gray stones warm in the long light.

But for him, it is different. He tries to figure it out, then gives up and just holds me, a daughter thing with hair like a storm cloud and a round, sturdy body, all of her as amazing as a bumper crop. He stares to the west, turning in his mind toward what to do about bugs or blight or which fertilizer to use. He is waiting for my mother; perhaps we both are, but his arms hold me in this hollow place where love is set, comes loose from its notch, and is replaced with something more precious.

SUMMER

We run wildly through it, up the hills behind the farmhouse, through the orchard and down to the back forty, where a fenced pasture with a fresh-running creek offers an unfettered paradise for my two rangy brothers and me. My little sisters are still that—too little, but we three risk barbed wire, grumpy bulls, and muddy lowlands for a slip of stream curving like a silver sickle through rough acres. In a narrow creek bed, crayfish, frogs, turtles, and small fish grow for the single purpose of being captured with makeshift poles and tattered nets. With the energy and will of beavers, we construct dams of sticks and mud only to see the greater will of the stream wear them down in hours. Where the current carves pools around large stones, we cool our dirty feet and scratched legs in cedar-stained water. We splash our faces, munch watercress, eat brown-sugar sandwiches and sliced apples from worn paper bags.

The bawling sound first whiffs out from the eastern pines that form a margin between pasture and true swamp, a green and hummocked boundary that we dare each other to cross but have not been actually able to do. We hear it again, rising and fading with the wind. We lift our heads, listening, sniffing like the animals we are; we drift into scrubland so poor even the pines look thin.

In the pines the world changes. Their sound is lonely, opposite ours. Talk is our chittering thread, running through the hours, pulling us tight. Pine words are low, slow, and dark, strung on wind that exists nowhere but in their boughs. As we walk into the pine stand, our skin cools. We turn quiet, stepping on the lichen until we round into a sandy clearing. She is standing, head low and tongue hanging. We watch the cow's rib cage heave. Tom announces, "She's gonna throw up."

I'm not so sure. I am just old enough to know that babies come from somewhere inside. I remember my mother's last pregnancy with my baby sister, Patti. I am sure enough of this to contradict him with big-sister authority. "Nope. She's having a calf."

The cow labors, breathing heavily, and bawls again, so loudly that we all step back.

"She doesn't look like she's having a good time." This from Rick, who figures things out.

"Is it supposed to hurt like that?" Tom asks. Since I have established myself as the expert and they are pretty certain this territory is exclusive to girls, they turn to me.

Although I am growing up on a farm, in the kind of animal openness where eggs hatch in your palms and pups are born in the mudroom, specifics are in short supply. The look of this cow seems alarming enough that bravado leaves me. I resort to honesty.

"I don't know."

"Then we better get Dad." My brothers move as one, small legs churning through the scrub.

I stay as long as I dare. At first, I talk to the cow as I have heard my father talk to riled horses: "Hey there, hey now, it's fine, just fine." And the phrase: "Easy now, easy there." Then I try to sing her some odd lullaby, a remnant from a grandparent. But after a short time the cow swings her head with a such an accusing look that I lapse into silence. Finally, her distress seems so clear that I think she may die. I leave her then, running through grasses and wetlands until I meet my father and my brothers coming back with twine and a switch.

My father follows us into the pines. When he sees her he says, "Got to get her moving." Is this knowledge or lore? But he ties her and pulls. She refuses and lows so loudly my hands sweat. We push and lash until at last she stumbles forward and waddles slowly out of the pines and across the pasture. We come to the creek, and there she halts. She will not cross but stands her ground despite my father's slap across her rump and my brothers' yelling. She settles in the mud as though its coolness finally eases something in her, and after long moments of convulsive pain she strains through a long cough of distress and raises her rump. A small black-and-white bundle hurtles with a gush from her backside. There beside the stream, we watch this Holstein thing torn from its slippery sack. We watch her tongue lick clean the tousle of bones and hide. Where he was brisk before my father is gentle now and we are quiet, watching to see if it will live, for we have all seen death births—cats and pups and even once a baby bull.

But this bundle kicks a little, trembles, thrusts itself upward. It is indeed a calf, and we look at one another and giggle. A small calf, wobbly but leaning forward, nuzzling. My father reaches down and places his fingers in its mouth; the calf sucks on them. He leads it to the udder, pulls his hand away, and lets its nose find the long, milky nipples. It raises its head and, tongue reaching, suckles with such insistence that the cow grunts. We watch, our wildness having run its course, our play tempered by our father's hands and face, full of purpose and intent on the calf. After a long time, he lifts the creature in his arms and begins the walk back to the barns, where all animals are housed until they must die.

I shiver through the grasses, trailing the boys and my father and the cow, now calm and unremarkable. I think of the creek, how it wears down whatever is in its way, no matter what we put in it to stop its force. In the moments I was alone with the cow, I saw the force of her contractions, how this work of hers could not be stopped, how she mooed and heaved but what was to happen would happen, how her voice was like the creek too, that sound of something wearing down, that held her death alongside the birth of the calf, and went on and on, the only thing that fought the river of her pain, so that they were two things, side by side, a thing that had to come, a thing that had to be mouthed and bellowed to the world. And I thought of my mother and how she held herself in our neighbor's kitchen just before my sister was born, how she was hard to know inside the mouth of her discomfort, holding her voice until the end when I heard her ask my father, in a low moan, to *take me in*. I pull the grass and see how one stream, one voice, is connected to another, calf coming and baby coming, and though I do not have words for what makes it so, I know these small joinings touch something that those words, not even the bellow without the words, can never touch.

First Scar

An empty hay wagon in a field off the end of the driveway.

I am running down the wide lawn on a bright day, running toward the barnyard, where I will climb a fence and run some more, or talk to myself, alone in some field. I am running across the green oval and down over the gravel driveway and into the longer grass where the equipment is parked. The men have pulled in a tractor and a hay wagon, one of those wagons that they have constructed in the workshop right on the farm with Dad bending over the welding machine. The back of the wagon is bound with a rough iron lip, framing the planks of the bed.

My eyes are open. I can see everything a girl running down a hill should see: the wagon coming closer, its dimension changing. I see it clearly, the bed of the wagon, the iron strut at the corner where the iron piece was cut raggedly. I see the way it juts out. I must turn, but I am running downhill. I do not judge the distance with the keen eye of my brothers. I do not judge at all.

But the body knows. And veers. But not enough. The open-ended strut that protects the wood of the flatbed reaches, as it should, for my face. I do not stop; I am stopped by a sharp blow against my brow. I feel nothing, but my sight goes in a wash of red. I feel vibrations in my teeth and tongue, an unsound of a scream that runs too fast inside my head, inside my cells.

My mother comes running from the house, out from under the silver maple, out from shadow, down to the open field. She uses the towel she carries to press and hold and stop the blood. The iron has been kind; it sheered open an inch of skin just above my left eye, exactly where the protrusion over the socket protects the eye. The cut is deep and bleeds profusely but runs along the bone. She tells me that is *a blessing* as she salves, butterflies, shakes her head at my clumsiness. She looks at the corner of the wagon to make sure there is no rust, then soothes me, murmuring over and over, "No harm done."

The wound heals. At first it is the only thing I see in the mirror, the jagged scab cutting through the brow. But over the months it fades, becomes a secret word on my face that few people discover unless they are willing to look closely for a long time. It is there but is a mostly forgotten thing, written on a moment in the past—the way sharp corners pull at me and I run into them and nothing can stop me—except something that sticks out, so abrupt it can tear a face open, the word for *momentum*.

Picture Girl

The boxy room of the Cleveland School is larger than the one at Kelly School, and there is more of everything: more chairs at the front, more coats on the hooks in the mudroom, a blacker blackboard, a dirtier floor, colder air. The desks are set little-to-big in rows. The bathroom is connected at the back, but it stinks, my mother says, because it is not in open air. More kids. More erasers. The big boys are supposed to clap out the chalk against the wall of the building, but sometimes they slap the erasers against our jackets hanging in the mudroom, causing a ruckus. The days feel like the needle on a record player slowing down because a clump of dust is dragging on it.

I sit in the row of first and second graders. We are doing numbers. I can recognize them and I can count a little, but they are not interesting to me. They mean only one thing. How can that be? Instead of counting, a big girl who helps little kids with their numbers is showing me how to draw a picture. It is one I love, the face of a girl with long hair, a turned-up nose, and lips the shape of a heart turned sideways. The face is like the faces of the pretty women on the Farm Bureau calendar in the back of Blackmer's store. The big girl loves this picture too. We look at the picture girl at recess. She is almost real and we want to be like her. So the big girl—is her name Marcia?—draws her, and we sit together at the same desk and look down together at the picture girl. The drawing looks back at us sideways. Marcia says that if you can draw really well, you can make the eyes of the drawing follow you, like the saint pictures in church. Her drawing doesn't do that, but still it is so beautiful that we stare. The drawing stares back. Sometimes it seems as though there are three of us.

I want to draw this picture.

Marcia, the big girl, lifts her pencil and makes the exact same lines over the lines of her drawing. As she copies, her lines turn darker. Then she tears out a clean page of notebook paper and places it over her thick drawing. She says, "Watch." When I look I can see the lines of her drawing showing through the new sheet. She says, "Now you trace."

"Trace?" I ask.

She takes my hand and helps me follow the faint show-through lines with my own pencil. The face from the old page slowly becomes the face on my page. I am so happy I giggle. She puts her finger to her mouth in a *shush* so we won't get caught. She gives me her drawing to trace and then goes away to geography lesson with the big kids.

I love tracing. I love seeing the shadow of the pretty girl's face appear on my page. I watch the nose and lips take shape, even the lines where the hair looks like more hair by copying a lot of lines next to each other. Through every numbers lesson, I draw the beautiful face with the heart-shaped lips, looking at the lines as I draw them, as her face becomes clear instead of faint. It amazes me, the way this picture of the girl shows through each time, how she gets more real as I trace her. I keep them all, every single picture, stuffed under the lid of the desk that opens like a mouth.

But the paper can slip. If I don't hold on to it tight, it shifts, though I can't always tell. When I lift it, excited to see my drawing separate from hers, the face is half right and half wrong, as though someone cut it and tried to put it back together but couldn't. I try to get it right, but I make it worse. I am trying to keep the sheets straight, one on top of the other, corners even. My shoulders round over the paper. My finger gets a red bump from holding my pencil so tightly.

The Mexican boy who sits across from me coughs hard. I forget the pretty-girl picture because I am distracted by his cough. It sounds like a terrible song, high and low, something akin to the old organ at church or water in a drain. The teacher looks up too. The boy's name is Pedro, after Saint Peter, he once told the class, but everybody laughed. He has the same brown skin as the Mexican family who work for us, so I think he is from Texas. He speaks only a few times a day. But the cough speaks louder than his voice.

The teacher looks at him. He gets up, goes into the bathroom, and we hear him cough until the teacher sighs, walks to the back of the room, and waits for him. When he comes out, they talk at the back of the room. She asks questions quietly and he answers in one or two words, even more quietly. I wish she would talk to me like that. When he comes back to his seat, he is not coughing anymore, but his nose is crusty and bleeds where the skin is broken from his blowing. He holds a brown paper towel to his nose, but it doesn't catch the slow drip onto his chin. When he rubs, it bleeds more. I look down at the drawing of the beautiful girl and I scuff the floor. Her face is crooked. I take a fresh sheet from a spiral notebook, watching the tiny little holes let go from the metal as I do. I begin to trace the picture girl again, trying to go to that place where she is appearing on the page, so pretty and perfect.

A few days later Pedro falls asleep at his desk. He is breathing through his mouth. Drool forms a small pool under his cheek. His face is flushed the color of berries. The teacher always wakes up kids who sleep by tapping them with a ruler on the shoulder, but she lets him sleep. When he wakes, he runs his sleeve across his face and with the same sleeve wipes his desk. He looks around to see if anyone has seen him, then takes out a book. He reads slowly to himself, shaping the words as if they were something to be careful of in his mouth. Sometimes the teacher watches him.

Is it then that she does the thing with the rough brown towels we use to dry our hands? She pulls out a handful from the bin and makes them wet. She runs the water over them, crinkles them up, wrings them out. When she has done this a couple of times, she hangs them on a short line over the grate of the oil stove where we sometimes hang wet mittens, though it takes a long time for them to dry. They smell like must, a word that has two meanings. In the afternoon she takes down the towels and crinkles them again. They have become soft like the cloth napkins that my mother uses only for Easter.

The teacher takes these to Pedro's desk. She kneels next to the desk instead of bending over it, something I have never seen her do. She talks to him softly about the stack of soft brown towels. He listens carefully. She makes gestures with her hands like blowing her nose. Although he nods, he says nothing. I watch his face as she speaks to him. It is full of what my mother calls *courtesy*. But his eyes are tired. They want to close.

I want her to kneel by my desk too. I bang on my desk cover, feeling as small as a piece of broken glass.

When she is done talking with him, he takes the napkins and goes into the bathroom. We hear him blow his nose again and again. Something in the blowing makes him cough even more, but finally it stops and he comes out again into the room that has been listening. His face is like gray stone. He drops into his seat with a thud. With one hand he holds one of the towels close to his nose. He stuffs the rest in his pocket. I stare and do not realize I am staring until he stares back. He shakes his head and points to my paper. I look at the drawing I have been working on. The page has shifted while I was watching him. When I lift the traced page off, I see picture girl is crooked in the middle. I try to fix the lines by connecting them smoothly, but the mistake part gets thick and she is not pretty but like my reflection in a tin mirror at the fair that scared me. I try to erase but the eraser is damp and it makes a big pink and gray shadow on the page. I erase until the paper tears. I kick my feet; the teacher scolds.

At recess, I tear the page out and stuff it into Pedro's desk.

I spend all that afternoon, every moment I am not in a lesson, trying to draw the perfect picture of the pretty girl. If I get it right, I stare at her. For a little while I believe I am her. It is as though I am the picture. But it doesn't last. It is like feeling warm out of the bath; it goes away quick. I notice something uneven; I have to start again.

I am drawing what I believe is the perfect picture. I am slow. I am careful. I am thinking about the face. Pedro opens the top of his desk to take out a book. I see him unfold the bad sketch, look at it, look at me. He doesn't do anything. He just looks at me. I look at him, at his face, all the lines around his eyes, the straight nose, which is red but if it were not would be like the prince's in the "The Snow Queen." His eyes, like dark flat water. He stares for so long that I look away. I look down at the drawing of the pretty girl. I pull away the master. The drawing makes me want to suck my thumb. There is too much white space, too much that is empty. I wonder if I copied every line, but when I put my drawing over the darker drawing to check the trace, what is underneath is invisible. I have copied it correctly but something is wrong. Why don't I feel like I am the picture?

It must be his fault. He should go away.

Is that the day Pedro stops coming to school? No one says anything about him, but his desk is empty after that. I learn that a lot of families go back to Texas when the apple season, the last crop, is over. I think Pedro's family has gone back, but then one day a short woman with dark eyes the same as Pedro's comes to the school. The teacher cleans out Pedro's desk and gives her some books and says she is *so sorry.* I think about his face and the bad drawing I gave to him.

I keep drawing picture girl, more and more, but it never works. I can't get her back.

One day the teacher catches me drawing. She has seen enough. She makes me clean my desk in front of everyone. There they are, page after page of picture girl's face. I pull them, rumpled, out of the small desk, one after another and stack them, the same face with small variations of hair, eyes, the sideways hearts for lips. The teacher asks, "How could you waste so much paper?" She makes me throw them in the trash. She says, "Do your arithmetic."

But she misses Marcia's original drawing. I keep it in the big book of stories. Sometimes I sneak the drawing out and stare at it. The lines have been traced so many times, grooves mar the paper. I can feel them, like roads on a map, with my fingers. When I lift the now frayed sheet and hold it to the air, some light comes through the lines. It doesn't look clear and whole as it once did. I know, with a good shake, the face will come loose like a cut-out paper doll and flutter, a separate thing, onto the floor. It isn't the face of someone hurt, or lonesome, or any of the things I saw in Pedro's face, in the face I could not be kind to but cannot forget. It isn't about anything but some worn-out lines. It could never be me. I put it back and forget about it and one day it is gone.

MIRACLE

Nobody walks to school now. We stand on the sides of our unnamed gravel roads in the knapweed and sedge and wait for the bus. Crystal Valley, Elbridge, Twin Bridges, and Walkerville kids scuff and wrestle in the cool September mornings, watching the road where each of them lives. Imagine the bus. Imagine the distant growl just before it breaks the crest of the north rise, that rough engine straining in the sand. Imagine the bus, appearing like a yellow ghost, billowing down the road, dust rising in the sunlight as it stops in its own cloud. The door swings back into a dirty fold. Lonely already, we climb up the too-high steps. If we are lucky, we find a red vinyl seat that is not taped. We sit through the long ride—the bus's gears roaring, door swinging open—for an hour through the farthest reaches of this new district. The bus meanders along gravel roads, stopping at the plain black or silver mailboxes that tack our small farms to who we are. The seats crowd up with small strangers, each pressed into the one new school outfit the family has been able to afford. Imagine wondering who will sit with you. You hope it will not be one of the bigger boys who will call you a little knucklehead. You are relieved when a girl who may go to your church sits down with her new Mickey Mouse pencil box shining in her hands. Imagine, after the long ride, all the buses lining up like monster caterpillars before this new house of school. Imagine climbing down, walking up a sidewalk lined with dirt. Imagine the wide metal doors propped open with shiny rubber stops.

Walk into the long hall that has nothing to stop it until you come to the end of the building.

Imagine tile floors instead of wooden planks, slim radiators traded for coal and oil stoves, light spilling through big metal-framed windows instead of the old double-hungs. Imagine separate bathrooms for boys and girls with four stalls each and a floor made of thousands of tiny smooth chips. Walk in one morning in September and watch it be real to children who have never seen the world so big.

The first morning, my clothes feel small.

Overwhelmed, I look for the room that will be mine with all the other second and third graders. The noise echoes like tiny lightning strikes all down the halls and I think that I am lost. But someone's mother, standing in the middle of the hall, bends and asks, "What grade you in?" I answer; she points. I move toward the door, into a line of children whose names are checked off by a woman in a pretty blue skirt and white blouse. She has new shoes with high heels. She says, "I'm Miss Robin." I stop at the door, peering in the way an animal nuzzles before it enters a den. The classroom is square, clean, and larger than the one-roomers. Every blackboard is green, not black; the chalk is yellow, not white. The teacher's desk is creamy brown, the small desks have shiny tops and no one's name is carved into them. They do not have even the little ink holes in the corners where we used to put dandelions. There is a tiny bathroom all our own in the corner. The lights are secrets, long skinny bulbs all across the ceiling of the room.

I am one among many, all about my size. We collect, quivering and tumbling like puppies, eager and afraid of this new place, this bright room with its wall of windows and the smell of something so raw it burns our noses with its sharpness. I look out the window to a playground as large and wide as a field. It is barren, still rutted in places with the cleated prints of big machines, but there are three swing sets, a thing called monkey bars, and space—one of the boys announces—for *two baseball fields.* Beyond that, even with all that change swirling around us, are the fields—our world still cradled in a patchwork of fields, the boundaries of this new house. And here also, the days stretch before us like new stones in a field.

Rain falls hard, a dirty chiffon across the already muddied playground. I stare at it through sprigs of skinny marigolds struggling in their paper cups on top of the radiator. They are part of a "speermint." Behind me, a classroom of Jensens, Smiths, Villadsons, Blackmers, Cutters, and Clarks—all children whose names I can say, first and last, after all these months—are playing the puzzle game, the math game, the cut-out game where you get to use paste, which I like because it is as salty and buttery as popcorn. This is *activity period.* After that will be recess, then the part of the day I dread, the reading group. I am with the second graders, not the third graders, which is my grade. I have given up on reading. I have decided I cannot read, and besides that it is not worth doing. It is like hitting something you cannot see, like the bird that flew smack into the new windows. It thought it could fly in, but it hit and dropped hard onto the gravel and sat in the dirt looking stupid. Maybe it died.

But there is no denying that I will continue to be taught even if I have decided not to learn, though I have learned some things. My mother has been teaching me, on the teacher's advice, something called "sounding out" words. I have gotten better, but I am still at the beginning levels. Still I don't understand the Dick and Jane words. There are too many strange things about the words and the pictures that go with them. Why sidewalks? They happen in cities and they are always clean. How do they do that? And why a dog named Spot? Not Dutch. Or Hunter. Or even Biscuit. What is it that the dog is really supposed to do? He doesn't hunt. And that red wagon? What is that all about? Don't they have a wheelbarrow? And nothing magic ever happens like in the fairy tales my mother reads. There is no swamp to be lost in, no Snow Queen to battle, no prince to climb the vines, not even Superman. As if that weren't enough, there are now flash cards added to the lessons. Can you say this word? *Jump.* This one? *Run.* But they don't mean anything, and I stare out at the playground, where the swing sways in a gust of wet that looks like a cape.

After lunch there will be story time, the best part of the day. We put our heads down on the new light surface of the Formica desks and listen to a whole chapter of a big book. Our teacher has read some good ones to us. There was the Oz story. And then in the multipurpose room we saw the movie, which was not as scary as the book and Judy Garland sang the songs. My favorite is "If I Only Had a Brain," which everyone thinks is funny.

What I do with my time in school is listen, not to lessons but secretly to other people's talk. When my mother discovers this, she scolds me but I learn a new word—*eavesdropping.* I am not to do it because it takes away a person's privacy. I do try not to listen, but voices draw me in. I listen to how soft the voices are and who they are aimed at, and I can tell if a secret is being told. So I listen. I am staring at the marigolds with their misshapen leaves, but I am hearing the Birdy girl tell about the car accident she saw at the corner of their road, where someone drunk ran into someone else and the drunk got thrown through the windshield. But he didn't die; he got up and walked away. "My daddy said just dumb luck," Sally Birdy says to Lydia, a girl so pretty I stare at her during our spelling lessons. "To be born with a head that hard. The drunk guy just got up and walked away."

I am good at this, looking in one direction, listening in another. I know if I turn and ask them the details I would like to know, they will turn away and not talk to me. It is because I cannot read. I believe this deeply. It makes me feel like night when no one can see it but it is there.

I am in third grade. I am supposed to know how to read, but I have few friends because I don't know how. They see words differently than I do. They see, when I stumble on the word, *then,* a time word. The teacher says, *then* Dick did this, *then* Jane did that. It has to do with order of things. But it doesn't sound the way it means. It doesn't really have much of a sound at all. I can't remember the *th* part, how come it doesn't sound like the *t,* which I know from sounding out. And the *e* is not the same as the two *ee's* in the word *seem,* which I learned in spelling. I am fascinated because that word, *seem,* starts to get at the world. Things *seem* one way; they *are* another way. Long *ee's* are like a soft knife that separates what happens from something else. Besides, I like the way things *seem* better than the way they are, and the word, with its long sound, means the way it is. That makes it easy. But *seem* doesn't count; it is not in the Dick and Jane books. *Then* is, and I don't get *then.* I am the only one who doesn't, and no one will pat my hand and say it is all right. Even my mother now sits with me at night, showing me the flash cards, which have sharp corners. From that, I know it is not all right.

I sit with my head in the curve of my grimy elbow, my fingers playing with my ear. The tiny alcove at the corner of the room is open to the rest of the room. One side is created by the window with the radiator beneath and the marigolds. But the other two walls are shaped by old bookcases, tall, heavy wooden ones brought from one of the one-rooms when they closed. The cases are built of heavy, dark wood, with the wide swirl in the grain that seems to have faces in it. In the space, two small chairs. I sit on one and listen to Sally tell again the same story about the drunk. They sit a few feet away, in desks that face each other so they can have a board game between them. They giggle again about the drunk.

I feel like hot water all over. I turn and say, "You can't fly through a window and not get cut." Every time I see Gus in the hall, I know this for sure. I have seen how glass breaks, how it cuts. They stop and look at me. Then Sally says with a voice like Kool-Aid, "And you know so much?" They look at each other and giggle again.

I turn to the bookcase, pretending to search for something. The rain smats against the glass and runs down in little rivers. Someone on the other side of the room farts and the Cutter boy laughs. Paper tears and scissors snip. I hear someone open the paste jar. The tiny bathroom in the opposite corner echoes with a flush. Chucky asks how long before lunch, which is a stupid question because it's just about recess, so that means

it's the middle of the morning. The teacher sighs at her desk; she's folding construction paper for Friday's one and only art project, my other
favorite time, which is still several days away. I stare at the books, letting
the sounds come in like slow wind.

For the first time, I notice that some of these books are old, with
dark-colored covers, different from the too-bright readers we use for lessons. Some books have gold lines around the titles. In some, the leather
is raised like my mother's fairy-tale books. There is one, small but pretty,
that catches my eye, and I slip it out. It has a paper cover over the dark-
red hardcover. A picture of two kids on the front, a girl with blonde hair
and a boy with darker hair. Their heads lean together and they smile out
from the cover. I trace the title. Did the teacher read a book like this?
Not exactly like it but maybe with the same little girl. I figure out the
name: *Honey Bunch*. Then some more words. The two kids are Honey
Bunch and . . . Norman. He is her friend. I glance sideways. Carla stares
me down. I turn back, open the book.

I'll show them. I can *seem* to read.

The middle of the book has few pictures, so I know it is a hard-to-
read book. I put my finger on a sentence and focus on the words. I can
tell something bad is happening because of the picture. Honey Bunch is
in the woods, a big woods like ours, and she is running . . . and trying to
. . . she is trying to help a rabbit, a wild rabbit . . . but she gets . . . lost. I
back up a few lines. There is something about a wheel rolling away and
her running, something dangerous is about to happen and she must be
rescued. No. She must be very clever and rescue herself. I go back, set the
sentence right, figure out the detail. Go at it again.

She is in big trouble.

The teacher taps the bell on her desk, but I don't hear it. I have
to find out what happens and so I am slowly fingering the words, skip-
ping hard ones, moving over lines as fast as I can. Only when she speaks
sharply do I fold the corner of the book as I have seen my mother do
when the Snow Queen story was too long—though Miss Robin says
not to. I hide the book on the bottom shelf so no one will take it. I walk
into the circle of small chairs that forms the reading group. I stumble on

every word, not concentrating, not thinking about the lesson at all and finally I decide not to talk. I am silent every time Miss Robin calls on me, and she finally gives up too, so I sit with the book open in my lap and don't cause any trouble while she works with the ones who will at least respond. Everyone is cranky, including her; she hasn't had a cigarette since breakfast, and all these children have to stay in because of the rain.

The lesson ends early and we go to geography, which at least has those blue-yellow-green maps and is about places I have never heard of that might or might not really be on earth, depending on which kid you talk to. Sally's older brother tries to tell me that parts of Africa are just made up, that there is no country where there are only colored people. Miss Robin says they are to be called "Negroes." The boy snickers but keeps his mouth shut. Today it is Mexico we are studying, and someone says that's where all the "Spics" come from and the teacher says, "No, they are Mexican people," and two brown-skinned boys in the back duck their heads. Patty Turner leans over and pats one of the boys and shows him the place in the book.

But I am only partly aware, only waiting for it to be over.

Somewhere inside me there is a seeming world that is more real than this one. It is the world Honey Bunch and Norman are living in. Where it is not raining through recess but they are in danger with a wagon, no, it's a cart, bright green with new seats. There is a pony involved, trouble with that wheel. Their danger is more real than what is happening in this cinder-block classroom in the middle of Elbridge Township in a remote part of Oceana County on the edge of old farming country.

The rain slows, turns to mist, stops by lunchtime. Although it is muddy, the teachers will walk the students out and around the building three times, keeping them out of the puddles but getting rid of some of that crowded-in energy. I make my way through the line of children pulling on spring coats. Miss Robin turns, her face tired like my mother's.

"Can I stay in?"

"You need to get some exercise." She pulls slim rubber boots over her patent-leather shoes. She stares at me. "Why do you want to stay in?"

"I want to . . . I want to practice reading." This is a lie. Isn't it?

"*You* want to practice reading?" She sighs but lets me stay in.

I sit in the small alcove for all of lunch, running my fingertips over the lines, mouthing the words that are coming now to the surface like fish. I study a word and the words around it until they move toward me like shards of metal drawn to the small magnet in science class. Once they are there, they do not let go. I move through the pages, from one simple adventure to the next. I understand this story the way I have understood when listening to fairy tales. Something is happening, taking shape. No one in a perfectly clean dress is standing on a sidewalk saying, "Look. Look." They are doing something that I want to know about, something that I want the way I want my father to laugh. The word *plot* is years away, but if you had asked, I would have said simply, "I need to know what happens." *What happens to them?*

What happens to me is that the pieces come together in a few hours; they come together during the lunch and afternoon recesses and the bus ride home, where for the first time I don't care that no one wants to talk to me because Honey Bunch has just been found by a strange boy in the woods. I don't care because suddenly words are there and—this is something I can't say, only feel as I read—I can at last forget them.

I am too young to know what a miracle is except for the biblical versions that have been read to me, full of fire and floods. I don't know that a miracle's setting might be as ordinary and plain as a small alcove of books, as simple as wilting marigolds blooming after all. The mind hits an invisible window, which, instead of the thud and drop, breaks open. All the pieces fly apart and then come back together into an order, so that a child can move through shards of language, watching them come into their places. A body, dizzy with something intoxicating, moving through, tumbling, rolling, could rise safe and walk, dumb with luck. What "seems" becomes real. Fire and flood. Right then.

A few weeks later my mother comes home from parent-teacher conferences, where she has just learned that Tom in first grade has told his teacher, an old friend of hers, that his mother's favorite word is *Oh shit*. She blushes when she tells my father, and he laughs so hard he has to get a beer. She almost forgets the other thing. But the next afternoon she sits with me at the table after supper, after the pots and pans have stopped banging their old song. There is a moment when she simply looks at my dirty face and round body and messy hair. I feel itchy. And then she says, "Your teacher says you can read. That . . ." and she hesitates, for it is an odd way for her to say it, "that you've become a reader."

And I don't remember my answer, don't remember the *then,* the kind of day or the clothes or my brothers and sisters, who are surely the color in the mist of this moment. But I am already in a different one, the moment of naming. It is my mother's statement that gives reading its personal identity. Something I didn't have takes up a permanent place in me. Something of who I am grows right there, in that word. I stare and stare into my mother's quiet eyes. I could swim in what is there, I could die in what is there, a huge window that I have never seen before, wide and open, revealing—what is it—a field full of books with hundreds of pages, all humming with the forward motion of words, and one word above them all. Reader. Reader.

The Sacred

It's called a Michigan basement, the space that lives under our house. To get there, I must walk down a wooden structure that is more ladder than stairs. It trembles like a tree in the wind. The stone walls are crusted with soot and cobwebs. A single dim bulb funnels bland light into the middle of three gaunt rooms. The coal bin and stoker play pawns to a stove that stands, monster in a sand pit, overseer to the bowels of our house. Down there, old guns and fishing gear hang on the walls like ancient skeletons; tangled ropes and broken tools are stacked like forgotten bones, and always, always, there are the ghosts of empty Mason jars.

I am afraid of this understory: scent of potato decay, oily odor of coal, the rank smell of hounds my father houses there when temperatures plummet. I am afraid of the stoker, its cantankerous roar, the click and shuck of the furnace as the blaze heats in its innards. Most of all, I am afraid of the silence, how everything is muted and excluded from the ruckus upstairs. For though I love quiet, I can sometimes distinguish a silence that is dangerous from another that is safe. The cellar silence is a landscape of dust, webs, dirt, and stone that makes me want to throw up. If I am not careful, it will erase me.

But in the corner of the basement, a rough-boarded pantry partitioned in the incense of must is the secret place of my mother's alchemy. A fruit cellar. In that shelved alcove sits all our harvests in quart jars.

In the morning, my mother will look over her kitchen, then out into the fields, surveying the day, reading it like a fortune-teller. She will think about which harvest we are in and who is helping with it. She will speak to my father in quick questions, and she will understand what must be done first and second. I see her standing at the cracked window with the coffee cup half up to her lips. She is figuring out the food first. She is remembering what is in the refrigerator, how much milk, how much butter. She is thinking about the almost too ripe tomatoes in the baskets outside the back door. Finally, she is recalling what is in the blue jars in the fruit cellar. From these slim beginnings, she will speak a plan, weaving a day of meals in among the washing, the fields, the sewing, and hoeing. She must feed us all. She must keep the world straight. I think she is what my father calls brave.

"I'll need two quarts of canned fish." I see what she knew already. It is Friday and so there will be fish patties. "And a pint of beets, a quart each of peas and rhubarb. And if the potatoes are not sprouted, bring enough for a meal." And as she says it I can see how it will go. She thinks and speaks and moves and many things happen. How does she do this? This is a mystery like the mysteries in the rosary, something no one understands so we have to contemplate it.

She knows when to pull radishes and how to recut and sew one dress from another. She knows how to make and remake. She knows things that no one else knows.

I am the oldest so I am the one most often sent to bring up the canned jars of peaches, pears, green beans, corn, pickles, beets. I am just coordinated enough to carry four quarts, two in each arm. I want to carry four because then I have to descend fewer times. All winter I carry them up full and down empty until the empty jars, like insect carapaces, line the floor with blue shadow.

In the summer the pattern shifts. I am sent to collect the empty jars, riddled with winter flies and coal dust, and carry them up to be filled with home-growns, everything from plums to beets, relish to jelly. We chop beans and husk corn and peel apples and all of it gets poured and capped and sealed into the womb of blue glass. She counts them as we work and remembers, adding them in her head until there are enough to outlast the cold: fifty-seven quarts of tomatoes; thirty-six of beans, squash, pickles; two dozen each of cherries, blueberries, grape juice. And all those peaches.

I am the carrier of both the full and the empty jars, the harvest and the emptying of the harvest. I try to be brave.

It is winter again. I have been sent for the assigned jars for the day's meals. I stand, thinking of my mother waiting for the jars. For all that she knows, how does she not know about this one thing? My mother sees everything, even things that no one else sees but are real. How does she not know about the cellar?

I stand at the top of the stairs. I brace open the nicked wooden door so that some daylight spills down the stairs. The musty air sweeps up into my face. I shift toward the wall just enough to feel the damp on my arm as my guide. I could touch the wall with its dark strings of web and soot, but my hands are full of glass. My feet feel forward and down three, four, five steps. With each step I stop to wait for the wood to steady. With each step the dark eats more of the light. When I reach the bottom, I stop again.

I have to do this part just right, an exactness.

I walk at a diagonal slowly into the charcoal dark so that the slim chain hanging from the bulb will touch my face or hands. When its coldness brushes my cheek, my body clenches like a small fork. I have to make myself reach up and pull. Only once do I miss it and walk into the shallow pit where the stove rumbles. The jars roll onto the sand. My breath sucks so deeply into my body it hurts.

When I pull the chain, it makes a rough little growl and the light pools dimly on the dark stone. Small puffs of dirt rise around my shoes as I move. Only a slice of light actually falls in from the larger room.

My shadow blocks even that. I force myself to bend toward the crates. I stack the four empty Mason jars in a bushel. Glass clinks its warnings. I straighten up, turn to the other wall draped with gray web so thick it is like letters on stone. I find the shelf where the jars of peaches stand like soldiers in tight rows. Twenty-seven quarts left, I know. I reach into the coombed nook, toward the sagging shelves, place my fingertips on the tin caps, press the top to check the seal—if the seal is broken I will be sent back—pull down two dusty quarts, enough for cobbler, and one jar of blackberries for breakfast cereal.

And without being asked, a jar of pickles for my grandfather.

I squint into this stone night, check for spiders on my shoulders and mold in the jars. I look straight at the ghosts, say a small prayer, take several soft breaths and wipe my cheeks to make sure my face is dry, not wet, when I rise out of this place. My mother cannot see that I am afraid. I turn, place first one foot, then another in the delicate dust, then on to the steps, bringing up from this place of fear the pale yellow fruit of sunshine, bringing summer from the dark, promising that no one will ever know.

Except one day, after I have set the jars on the counter, she turns and catches something she has not seen, and she looks at me. She cups my chin in her hand. She is about to say something. Her mouth opens. Then I hear the baby cry. I hear the laundry flapping on the line. I hear the cherries ripening and the gray floor with its sand-tracked words scraping under our heels. I hear what she hears. She lets go of my chin without speaking. She has seen something she could not foretell and so could not speak to it. It scares her but she must not let it. This is how it will be between us for awhile, how we know each other: in sidelong glances, almost caught wishes and fears, in her bravery so old it is holy as a cellar full of food.

PEARLS

Lydia is small, slim as a sapling. She lacks the solidness that marks my family with big bones, fair hair, broad faces, stamps of dirt-farmer heritage.
She is a *brunette*. Her hair is long, thick, straight, and her hair ribbon stays
in her ponytail. She has a small straight nose and cheekbones that catch
light at the top and make shadows under. Her eyes are brown with flecks
like little fires. Her hands are little and pale. She wears nail polish, which
she takes off with something she calls *remover*. She has a pair of black patent-leather shoes that are too tight for me. She does not go to the same
church we do, but something called Methodist, which my mother says
not to talk about. But stranger still, when something happens to her, she
does not hide it. Nothing about her is like what happens in my family,
the way we quiet things. Lydia says things right out. When something
goes wrong, she will kick and say right out loud, to Miss Robin or to
anyone, "This is stupid."

I love her. She is only partly in love back.

In that school of many rooms, she makes friends easily. She talks to all the girls, flirts with the older boys. She has a big brother, Earl, who everyone likes. I am plain and sturdy and friends do not come to me. If my hair is beautiful to my father, if my aunt has said I have large eyes, I know they lie. There is only one beauty and it is Lydia's. And Lydia's beauty and Lydia's charm reigns in the classroom where, despite new books and the multipurpose room, despite the *consolidation* that was supposed to help everyone, luck comes to only a few.

Like Lydia.

"Rhinestones," Lydia whispers over the noisy, glistening necklace that belongs to her mother, "They're a kind of diamond. They cost a bunch." She tells me diamonds are what Marilyn Monroe, the movie star, sings about. She whispers *Oooh,*—her moist, private fourth-grade mouth wrapping around the sound. Her quick eyes look into mine, her face moves up and down in a slow nod. In her husky tones the word turns into cream and I know this is something big.

I look around to see who is watching, but my grade is absorbed with *collages,* something new from the art teacher—tearing up pages of magazines and old wrapping paper. They are pasting words from the newspaper, from headlines about the thing called *election* that is coming. But for me, even these bright colors, this spray of words, cannot match the rhinestone necklace in Lydia's hands, the look of inclusiveness in her face.

Lydia flaunts the rhinestones all morning, carrying the necklace like a delicate hanky in her chipped "Orange Flame" nails. She shows it to all the girls at recess, but because I am the one who most likes to fondle it, she keeps me close. We stand near the swing set at the edge of the baseball field and whisper about how bright it is, though she looks at me strangely when I tell her there are fairies in the sparkles. She waves at Earl, her brother, who sidles over, mitt still in hand, from the outfield. Earl buckles her legs from behind the knees and says, "Hey, sis." She pretends to hit him. I am so delighted I laugh too loud. No one in my family says, *Hey, sis,* not to me, not to anyone. They call you by your name, or a very good nickname that means something. You are never to say, *Hey* unless you are talking about what you feed to cows.

The necklace slips out of her fist, drops in the sand. He looks at it, then at her. "Ma know you got that?" he asks, cocky but not mad. Lydia picks up the necklace, shakes the dust out of it, and slips it into her sweater pocket.

"Yeah," she lies.

"Don't lose it. Be hell to pay." Earl lopes back to the outfield. We both know he will not tell. Lydia and I stand at the edge of the playground, autumn wind whistling through our skirts. She is looking at the sparkling strand between her thumb and fingers. For the hundredth time she drops it slowly into the palm of her hand. She watches me eyeing the rhinestones. She smiles, holds them out, tangled in her fingertips, and nods at the question in my eyes. When I lift my own palm, she lets them drop jewel by jewel into my hands where they make tiny ice-water rainbows against my skin. She laughs. I laugh too. We are two girls, laughing about something pretty.

But when I close my hand, they feel brittle, like holding broken glass. I am surprised at how sharp they are. They are set in metal and the edge of the metal feels prickly on my skin.

I do not feel the wind kicking up the sand at our feet.

When I tell my stories about Lydia, when I giggle at how Lydia swings so high her underpants show, my mother's mouth gets tight. She knows that I am attracted to defiance. She knows there is a thing called shame and it is real and it can place you outside the circle. But will she see what I need?

"Wouldn't you like to play with Wilma or Dianna?" These are girls from our church who would never steal rhinestones.

I shake my head, silent at last.

But she knows our farm is isolated enough that no little girls live nearby. The friends I make will be from school. She knows I have ached for a friend and have not found one. For a year I have buried myself in the books that were a relief at first but now seem too present. She worries that I live too much in that world. She needs help with sweeping floors and folding clothes. There are two little boys starting to run wild and two little girls who just want to be loved, and my mother knows already that if I am resentful I will be of little help with any of it. I hold my breath.

"Yes, you can play with her." But my mother sighs even as she gives permission.

I do not tell her about the rhinestones.

Stealing the rhinestones becomes predictable as church. They must be snuck out of her house, onto the bus, into the school, then snuck back at night. When she opens her pencil box and slowly lifts them, she is waiting for my *oooh*. And we smile together at how forbidden and delicious they are. When the dismissal bell rings, and she slowly slips them back into the box, among the pink erasers and the hopscotch chalk, I must witness.

We invent history. She tells me her dad gave them to her mother for her twenty-first birthday at a ball. I tell her they are from a queen's first date with a handsome prince. She tells me they were a Christmas present given under mistletoe and lights, and I wonder if Methodists celebrate Christmas differently because my father never gives my mother jewelry, just practical things like a stepstool that turns into a ladder so she can reach the high cupboards when she is cleaning. We practice walking up and down the hall as if it were a marble corridor. We will be princesses together. We run over the playground, taking turns holding the sparkling thing that separates us from the rest of the world.

The day she loses them, she is running fast through the sandburs and spindly grass to get to the swing sets before the fifth graders do. It slips from her pocket, invisible for all that flickering. When we are red-faced from pumping *as high as the sky*, we come down off the swings so happy we cannot catch our breath, and we pant, looking into each other's eyes.

In the brisk sunshine, I ask to see it again.

Her fingertips, smeared today with Scarlet Joy, sink into the pocket.

Her hand gropes forward, then back, searching the corners where pencil nubs and dried-out hankies gather. She fumbles in first one jacket pocket, then another. And back. She looks at me. I shake my head, wishing I could pull them out and say with surprise, "How did these get here?" I watch her face change the way ice cream collapses when it melts. She mutters, stomps, shivers out of the jacket, shakes it upside down. Nothing drops out and she stares, open mouthed.

We hurry back to the schoolroom. On the way, I try to put my arms around her as my mother would comfort me, but she pushes me away, scans the ground. She bends to pick up foil, an old cigarette pack. She shrieks whenever something bright turns out to be a bottle cap.

When she is in sight of Miss Robin, she turns, throws both arms around my neck, and sobs into my Peter Pan collar. Suddenly she can barely stand until she is comforted into a desk and Miss Robin is handing her tissues. Through her sniffles, she tells Miss Robin the necklace *cannot be lost but somehow is.* She says her mom *will kill her.* She says she is *overcome.* She nods miserably. It is all true. As recess ends and damp-faced kids file into the room, everyone can see it. *Overcome.* She braces her elbow on the back of her small chair. The heel of her hand supports her head. She lifts her perfect, tear-streaked face, pushes back her shining hair, and confesses to the assembled, "My mother's rhinestones have disappeared."

I love her with all my heart.

After morning recess, Miss Robin announces to the entire class that Lydia has lost *a valuable piece of jewelry.* The phrase, "valuable piece of jewelry" makes the necklace as important as a Boy Scout medal or winning the Christmas card prize. Miss Robin asks us to look for Lydia's lost rhinestones during our lunch break. Her tone is soft and gentle in a way I have never heard. Everyone in the room nods and agrees to be helpful, to be good *friends of Lydia.* Maybe we can find them for her, she says. More nodding. Then Miss Robin warns that perhaps we should not bring such important things to school, even to show around. She is not mad. She is using her you-made-a-mistake-but-it's-all-right voice. Lydia is smiling like the picture on a holy card. At lunch all of the other friends of Lydia—all the girls and even a few boys—come to help. They surround her desk and tell her they will find the necklace. She smiles small and they all smile big. No words have to be spoken. All through lunch, the girls and boys in our grade walk the playground hunched like turkeys over the dirt, looking for worms. No one finds it. Lydia is so upset she cannot do her arithmetic but must sit by herself, sighing loudly over Miss Robin's new box of tissues.

But during afternoon recess one of the big boys in Earl's grade, swinging high in the sun, spots the glitter of necklace near the steel base of a swing pole. He shakes them off and brings them into the room because by now the whole school knows. With something like a bow, a little bend and curve, he offers them to her and she is tears all over again and announces that he *saved her life*. Then all her classmates gather round her, telling her how glad they are, as though they have each found her sparkling rhinestones. Now her mom *won't be mad* and they were *glad to help*.

I want to be her.

I want to have people love me the way they love her.

The way to be loved is to lose something valuable.

The plain white cardboard box with worn edges nestles in the top drawer of my mother's dresser. She keeps the cover closed with a rubber band but the rubber band snaps off, the cover comes loose, and the pearls can be slipped into a jacket pocket like pebbles into water. The next day I climb off the school bus with my mother's single strand of wedding pearls. I know these are special because she has said they are "handed down." She wears them only for holidays, weddings, and baptisms. Once in her bedroom, I found her sitting on the edge of the bed, looking down at them, tangled in her fingers like a shoestring.

The strand of pearls is the only real jewelry she has.

In the bathroom before school I show them to Linda, thinking she will want to hold them, that she will giggle and hide them in her hand like it is a big deal to keep the secret of the pearls from the other kids. But when she picks them up, she looks at me sideways, then drops them back into my hand. She does not make the *oooh*. Then she sees my face and tells me, without smiling, that they are "pretty nice" and lets the bathroom door slam.

At recess, we race to the east corner where the ground is hard clay, good for jumping rope. I lag behind, panting as though I have run too fast. I drop the pearls into a big clump of burdock at the base of the black electrical pole, a place I can find again, then catch up to the girls who are already doing hot peppers and doubles.

There is no sound like the sound of saddle shoes hitting the ground in the double jump that is a heartbeat, that is the way we know we are alive. It is addictive and hard and then, over time, easy, and the rhymes are what we chant together to make us one when nothing else makes us one. But today, I wait. Near the end of recess, I finally raise my hands, waiting for the right moment, rocking my way in and there it comes, the quick leap. I am in the twirling sphere, up and up, *doctor, lawyer, Indian chief.* I reach into my pocket as I jump and grope around, mimicking Lydia's gestures of the day before. I miss a step and the rope tangles, stops. I stand in the middle, moving my hands from one pocket to another like flies swirling. I kneel down and run my fingers through the sand at my feet, and then, with a dozen little girls watching, set up the tearful wail, "Pearls. My mother's pearls. I've lost them."

Even though the rope has dropped, Lydia is waiting, hands raised, poised for the rope to resume its twirl. She is impatient to get into the circle of the heartbeat. She is small and quick and it's easy for her to jump all the jumps. She is rocking. She is ready. But my voice is so loud and squally that she stops, lowers her arms, and gives me a squinty look. She looks down where the rope is a quiet snake in the dirt, then up at me. I think she will come over and put her arm around me now, and everyone will follow. Instead she says in a voice so knife sharp my eyes smart, "What the hell is wrong with you?" The girls shift away from me, repositioning. They begin to spin the rope handles. The twirling whirs up in its slow spin.

I am outside the circle.

Lydia rocks, leaps, and starts doubles but goes on talking so quick I can't keep up, asking haven't I *learned my lesson from her mistake.* Then, breathless and jarred, to the girls around us, "Just some pearls, they don't even sparkle."

A bright fire laces through me. This is my friend, the girl I love, the girl everyone loves. But she is not doing what I thought she would do. She is jumping rope. Now Shirley wants in. Shirley's rocking, she leaps, and they double jump until Shirley misses and the rope tangles. The next girls in line step forward.

Lydia steps out, sees my face, "Oh, all right." She rolls her eyes, "I'll tell Miss Robin."

But Miss Robin seems as annoyed as Lydia and only grudgingly makes an announcement, *for the second day in a row a piece of jewelry has been lost*. She says in her scolding voice, "You children know you shouldn't bring valuable things from home. Perhaps I had better call some parents and let them know so we'll have no more of this nonsense."

The word *nonsense* is full of sandburs.

All morning, Lydia, who sits nearer the front than I, does not turn around to mock Miss Robin during the geography lesson. There are no secret sideways glances. No one speaks to me. What I have done dawns slowly.

And what I must do.

At lunch, when enough kids are around to hear but none are so close that my discovery will look planned, I lean over the burdock at the base of the telephone pole and finger the pearls out of the dirt. I stand, hold them out so they drape over my hand, visible and loose. Putting loud delight in my voice, I announce, "Here they are. I found them. Oooh, I'm so glad. I want to thank everyone . . ." I look around the sandy, windswept grounds. Boys play baseball, girls loop through the monkey bars, little kids play Ring-around-the-Rosie. A few kids stare. One little guy from second grade says, "Tha's good," nodding to himself, then looks around to see if anyone noticed, goes back to playing by himself.

No one is really looking.

I find Lydia in line for Mother, May I. I show the pearls to her, thinking at least she will be glad, she will reach for them or touch my arm and say, *Hey*. But she looks at me and says, "Take your silly pearls and put them in your lunch pail so you won't lose them again." For the second time, my face feels like something hit it. I lower my head and walk into the long hallway of the school.

On the way home, as the bus empties out, I have a seat alone. I take the pearls out, unfold their toilet paper wrapping and run my fingers over them, trying to wipe the dust off. Even in the grimy light of the bus, they glow softly. They have colors in them, soft pinks and yellows. They are warm. If I look close, I can see reflections, like looking at something in water. They are round and easy as new peas in the hand. I lift them and taste, running the pearls over my tongue. The small beads are smooth, gentle in my mouth. They taste like the inside of early morning. But I think of Lydia, and how she did not think the pearls were a big deal.

They do not sparkle.

My mother is hanging clothes when I get home. I sneak the pearls back into their white box. I pull some underwear over the box. I leave the room, sit on the couch, and push my way toward sleep, just to get away from the red-faced memory, the feeling just before you cry. I wish my mother would come and tell me that Lydia is still my friend, that it will all be all right, that Lydia will like me. They will all like me. But she doesn't, and I already know she wouldn't say those things anyway. She would say something about one of the quiet, sweet girls who would be loyal and steady and would like me for who I am. I keep the secret of the pearls, separating for the first time the house of school from my mother's house.

Days later, we are sorting hand-me-downs in my mother's room. My little sister, Marijo, is trying on my too-small clothes. I am trying on clothes from my Aunt Stella in Muskegon.

Marijo is tired of too many sleeves too short for her long arms. She slides opens the dresser drawer. She can just see over the top. She reaches in and lifts the box.

My mother turns, "No, Marijo, you can't play with those." Marijo looks stubborn but my mother gently pries the box from her hands. She looks at Marijo's face, then opens the box. I hold my breath. She looks at them, lifts them, holds them in her hands. "See? These are pearls, the real McCoy." She uses her *this is special* voice.

"What's McCoy?" Marijo sounds the word carefully.

"Some things are fake. A real McCoy means it's real."

"Like rhinestones, huh?" I say, thinking I know.

"Rhinestones?" My mother looks like someone told a bad joke.

"Yeah, they're like diamonds."

"Rhinestones are glass."

"Glass?"

"A kind of glass." She considers. "Nice glass."

Something like a low cloud is in my head and I am trying to get it out. I look at her. I already know this. I don't want to know this. I love the glass, shining its broken rainbows. I love the thing that is not real, the girl who turns colors in the light, the friendships that will always cut me. I will never touch the pearls again. I believe Lydia will be my best friend forever. Won't she?

I watch my little sister pick up the pearls, remembering how they feel smooth as water. My mother puts her hands under Marijo's, then lets her hold them. "Be careful," she says.

I remember them in the sand.

"Are pearls better than rhinestones?"

"Yes." After she is sure Marijo will not yank them apart, she turns to hold a jumper up to my shoulders, sizing with her eyes. "Still too big. Maybe next year," she says.

"But rhinestones sparkle." I take the next dress from the box, trying to look interested.

"They're not real. The jewelers cut glass or crystal to look like diamonds. Pearls are real. They come from the sea." And the way she says this word makes me see the sea. I hold a little dress by a single button and she gently takes it out of my hands. She sighs. She fears already that I will be the kind of person to choose rhinestones every time, that I will choose the thing that flashes and not the thing that glows. She is right.

The House of Memory

Dear Mama,

This is the house of memory that I am in so deeply now I cannot move out or away and I have to walk through all the rooms. There is one room. I have to spend a lot of time here. You are here too. It starts with this: I wanted to find out what it was like to hold a boy. And I wanted to kiss. But it was not about sex. I have not even made the connection yet. But you know and you are afraid.

Although we may both be a little embarrassed, let me tell it so that you won't be afraid anymore, though there are some scary things for a mother. Mama, I tell the rest of these stories to erase the fears for both of us, to look at the house of our memory, both our houses, one inside the other, though I may never be sure which is which and that is fine.

I want to go to Lydia's house to play. I want to get away. I beg and beg until my mother says, "Yes, you can go."

One day I ride a different bus into the part of the county where my mother grew up, where the fields are a little richer and the road is paved.

We pass our little Catholic church with its Indian cemetery and its white cemetery and farther south is Ferry, which my mother won't talk about because *if you can't say anything nice, you shouldn't say anything at all.*

Lydia lives in Elbridge Township in a small green house that does not need paint. I meet Lydia's mother, and she says to call her Maggie and not Missus anything and I am amazed at this informality. She is a tall, lively redhead with a constant cigarette, thin quick hands, and a table of crafts where the dining room should be. She has a lower voice than my mother's and I think that Lydia speaks like her mother, with rhythms that are about secrets and skin. Her mother lets us sit at the cluttered table. She shows us how to make a new kind of Christmas ornament, with a foam ball that we cover with ribbons. We pin it with sequins and glitter. It is as pretty as anything I've ever seen. Lydia holds hers to her ear like an earring and we all giggle. Maggie is making the ornaments to sell but she lets me keep the green ball with gold braid because it was a little frayed. She talks on the phone. Once when she answers the phone, she sends us out into the yard. There is no talk of supper.

We run into the yard, a sprawling space with a row of chrysanthemums perking the edge. We run over grass, thrilled the wind has the promise of cold at its edges. I am crazy with my legs, with the sound of my own panting.

The big tree has a hollow place in the trunk where the roots spread like the arms of a chair to form a nook where one person can sit and feel the tree around his body like wings. Earl rests in the nook like he is someone. His mitt is on the ground next to him, the ball cradled in it. He has been playing catch with himself, throwing the ball up in the air and catching it. I stop, staring at him. He smiles. "We need some apples," he says. Lydia nods, runs down the yard to a spattering of trees where she scrambles through yellow grasses for the windfalls. He looks like a fairy-tale prince.

"You wanna try it?" I realize he means the tree chair. With all my heart. We trade places, but once I am settled, where I should feel as grand as he looked, the ground is hard, the bark rough, with flakes that scrape my bare arms. It is like looking at grass that should be pillowy but turns out to have sandburs in it. I get up, brushing my skirt.

But Earl knows things.

"Come here," he says. He sits up and gestures. I kneel, then turn and scoot back and he puts his arms around me and holds me. He is warm. Lydia comes back with apples, but when she sees us, her face changes. She throws away the apples and they roll into the mums.

Earl sighs like someone old, "Oh come on, *sis.*" He winks at her and waves his first finger to come. She giggles and wiggles in next to me. We shift and curl into a sweaty stillness—three kids in the hollow of an old maple. We sit like that for a long time, leaning back, watching the canopy of leaves just beginning to color in the September wind. The whole world feels golden to me.

But Lydia wiggles and picks at her polish. She sits up and stares at us. "You guys should practice kissing," she says.

Practice kissing!

"I'll watch." I think she means that she will watch the kissing, but I realize she means that she will watch for her mother, which tells me that kissing may not be something her mother would approve of. She rolls on her stomach and crawls cowboy style over the grass where she can see the house with its front window.

"Still on the phone," she whispers back to us.

The wind pushes slowly through the big maple branches overhead. It is nice to rest in Earl's arms, to smell the leather of his mitt on his hands. He is just holding me, and it feels safe like when my father holds me. We look at each other for a long time. After a while, he shrugs, picks up his mitt. He says, "Suit yourself." He gets up, brushing away the bark chips. He walks the walk of the big baseball players. He moves out toward their workshop where he throws the ball, over and over, against the gable.

Linda rolls her eyes, shouts, "You're it." Takes off running.

I know something is wrong because my mother has no sewing or laundry in her hands. She sits on the couch and gestures for me to sit next to her. She wants to know something. She looks at me.

"Do you like Earl?" This is about Earl?

"Uh-huh." I nod and look at her. Something gnaws at me.

"Does he play with you and Lydia?"

"Uh-huh, and he plays catch by himself. He can throw a ball up and catch it a hundred times."

"What else does he play?"

I don't know what she means and I can see there is something to this story that I don't know and that she does. I stay quiet, searching for the secret.

Finally she asks, "Does he ever play a kissing game with you?"

"No," but then I remember Lydia's suggestion. Practice kissing. Is this what she wants to know? She sees my hesitation like a hemstitch gone bad, something coming loose.

"One of the mothers told me that her little girl was playing at Lydia's house and Earl played a kissing game with her," she says.

I remember the tree. I remember the holding. We did not kiss. But I am in some field that is in between. Is kissing wrong? Why is she so serious? I think of kissing from the fairy tales. It would be nice, wouldn't it? And why did Earl play the game with someone else and not me? Someone else was at Lydia's? My hands turn cold.

"He didn't play it with me." I tell her quietly but she hears the unspoken part, though she can't clearly identify it. When I don't tell her what happened, she knows something is there that is not of her world but of her little girl's world. It scares her. It is not something she can be brave about. She tries to read what is there. I see her mouth close and the moment slips into the quiet of the living room. She leaves me, her hands still empty.

How much later is it that I am sitting on the bus as it lumbers through Elbridge Township, over the roads that pass through the orchards on the way to Walkerville? How is it that all the other kids have been dropped off and we are mostly alone and I am sitting in the brown seat with Danny Solon who is the only other kid on the bus and we kiss? We kiss more than once, maybe a whole bunch. I don't think about what I am doing. I do not think about the bus driver with his overhead mirror that sees all the way to the back. It is kind of fun but mostly silly, this practice kissing. It is just kissing. It wasn't nice like when Earl held me.

Afterward, the orchards whiz past and I notice the blossoms are just beginning but it is too early in the year. I know that they will freeze and my mother and father will worry about frost and I am half aware that I am very alone, though Danny is still sitting next to me.

This time it is the bus driver who tells. This time I do lie.

"I wasn't kissing." That wasn't kissing, was it? Not the way it was supposed to be. It was not like in the fairy-tale books where the princess wakes up.

My mother believes the adult, a bus driver who has no reason to lie, and this is the second time she has had to ask me about this thing that is like broken ice. In the fall, the first time the ice forms, the thin layer will not hold anything, but is there. It is glassy and sharp, but fragile.

Her face is like that. I look at it and I know that she knows. I ask the old childhood question. "Why?"

"Because you're too young." She says. She takes a breath. "If you behave like that, you get a reputation." She says it and there is a tiny crack in her voice.

"Reputation?"

"It's what people expect of you. That you'll be like that."

"So?"

"It's loose. It's cheap." Her voice is suddenly open water where there should be footing. "You don't want to be cheap."

It's a new way to use the word and it confuses me. I thought cheap was good, or at least okay because it means some thing costs less money. I look at her and the question shows on my face.

She takes a breath, keeps going. "If you give yourself away, it makes you worthless."

Here is a coldness like a sudden plunge, though why this should scare both of us so much, I don't yet know. But forever after, shame will be marked, not with its first flame-full flush, but with the feeling like a sudden drop that cannot hold the weight of being.

I didn't know I was giving myself away.

Oh Mama, with five, someone must always get diapers and baby clothes washed, someone must take the sheets and towels from the line, someone must sweep and hold the crying toddler. And then there are always the fields around us with their green and squalling demands. Even as a child, I can see the tiredness, the slow sense of loss growing, though I have no words for why the pans sometimes bang.

This is not criticism. I understand things now.

You don't know what to do about me. There is my resistance, my almost wildness, my little girl love affairs—and such overriding curiosity about the world and people. And beyond that, I make things up. I make up characters and play under the trees and create worlds that are not the worlds we live in. And sometimes I lie.

No wonder you worry. No wonder you become uncertain. No wonder you try to let go and keep close at the same time. No wonder you and Dad decide on a different plan. I tell you now, in all the things that followed, through all the strange passions and misconceptions of girlhood, I never doubted your love.

SNAP, SNAP

The milk spill slides across the table and makes a small white ocean. I run my fingers through it, smiling at Patti, my baby sister. Her mouth, a soft O, means she knows she did something wrong, but since no one is scolding yet, she may be able to get away with it. The kitchen door slams and my mother hurries in from the back yard, carrying rumpled but clean shirts still night-cool from the line. It is full dawn.

"Clean up the table please." She is brisk as she hands a tee shirt to Marijo, whose long arms snake up through the sleeves. She pulls a pajama top from Patti, who is almost too big for the high chair but too small for the table. I push a cloth through the milk and carry it sopping to the sink. She sighs. In the language of the house, the sigh means, *Can't you be of more help?*

"Hurry," she urges as I gather breakfast bowls. "Tom and Rick are out there already." *Out there* means the asparagus fields, where yet again they are preparing to pick this new crop that my father has taken a huge risk on, this new crop that we are harvesting in the June heat for the first full season after three years of waiting for it to mature.

This crop that could save a farm.

Crops have unwritten rules, sometimes loose and forgiving, but asparagus rules are uncompromising. Fast in spring heat, it pushes green spears up as quickly as half an inch an hour when the humidity and temperature are high. Asparagus must be picked tight and tender, as often as once a day. It is persistent in its call, for if the stalk grows too long, it spreads its tight-lipped head and opens at the tip. The value of a bushel drops to nothing. At the height of the season, if there has been rain, high warm winds, and full sun, a field picked before breakfast can be ready again after supper. We have been picking asparagus from this tract of sandy soil riddled with weeds and clay and killdeer for three weeks straight. We will pick for another three before the root tires and the stalks thin, the plant's signal to let it fern. A healthy field will yield every spring for twenty years. It is a crop to love for loyalty, resilience, and in the fall, when it spreads a gold canopy peppered with red berries, for beauty. But during the season, its primary characteristics are unrelenting persistence and absolutely necessary cash.

Marijo is eager, more good-hearted about this work than I am. Patti will be nestled into a tented crate on the asparagus picker where she will fall asleep curled on a dusty pillow. It will take six to eight hours to pick ten acres. I scuff my feet on the rungs of my chair. It is always the same, this field, these rows of green, the work of them. I want to read or play dress-up and act out fairy tales in the barn, anything but the spilled milk of work.

I cast about for ways out. Am I sick? Is there a pain in my tooth, my side, my heart? My mother moves quickly through the kitchen. Her back hurts. I can tell by the way she leans forward as she moves, but her forward motion is also relentless. I know this work will surround the day, as present as walls in a too-small house. I can see it in her face, her quick hands. "Come on," she says briskly. She sweeps up Patti. Marijo follows, singing softly to herself. My mother stops, looks at me, sighs again. I scuff my feet out the door, across the yard, out to the field, dreading heat, biting flies, dust, and a tiredness that has nothing to do with the body.

The field stretches over two low slopes. The truck is parked at the corner, where we always start. My brothers and the workers yank off and drop crates onto the picker, the mechanical platform we ride to make the picking easier. I lean against the pick-up fender, already hot from early sun. In the hot dust of the metal I draw a hangman, a new game I have learned. I look at the dangling stick figure. Trapped, captured, dead. Why is the world about this ash-colored dirt where everything is turning dry as old straw, demanding as hunger? What will I do with weeks of these green stalks ahead and after that tart cherries, pickles, hay, and how many other small or large green harvests from these damn fields?

The world has been too much the same, the end of school was the same, the summer days have been the same, the tasks are all familiar to the point of numbness.

My mother snaps her fingers. That sound.

They are all there, the Mendozas—the migrant family—two local women, my brothers. The engine of the picker starts with a puff of exhaust. My brother pulls it out over the rows. We ride, snapping the lush stalks and tossing them into bushels. It is another quick sound, like snapping fingers but sharper, and sharpest early in the morning, less clear later in the afternoon. Snap. Snap.

We settle into the long rows, a quarter mile of pebbled soil riddled with pools of hard clay on low ground. We lean toward the rows, our backs rounding under the heat. We bend to it like worshipping. On some level we do worship it, for the entire country is discovering the delicacy of these moisture-ridden stems. What was once a garden oddity or small-plot plant for country people is becoming common fare for the urban table. But for us, it is a daily vegetable, eaten every single day of the season. This too is monotony, right down to the way our pee smells.

Our hands are swift as small claws. We reach down into the crown of stalks and break the stem as close to the ground as we can. The stubs, which will grow half an inch even after the stalk is picked, will dry as the days pass. Late in the season, with a dozen or so broken stems at every root clump, the stems will cut our hands. By the end of the six weeks, our knuckles will look as though we have battled a small wild cat and lost. We will wear gloves despite the added clumsiness.

But *close to the ground* is also trick of weight. Asparagus is bought and sold by weight, and the weight of the stalk is at the base. We could dig our fingers in the dirt, or use knives as we hear they do in California, but this would unveil the white butts, the part below the ground, and that part is tough and inedible. For the best price, the stalk must be broken precisely at the surface of the dirt, where the stem is heavy but before the white butt shows. This is the most important rule. We all know it.

But I pick sloppily, breaking the stalk an inch or two up, leaving the weighty base, ignoring what I know, that in a week, the stems will maim our skin, the dirt will irritate the cuts.

We move across the field like a swarm of low-flying insects following the wide wings of a queen. The tractor thrums in the morning air. The dust rises in a low cloud. At the end of the first round, Rick counts his bushels.

"Fifty cents," he announces. He is a fast, steady worker and he keeps track carefully. We are paid a quarter a bushel, and all of us are included in this phenomenon of being paid. It is new to us, but my mother and father have explained this is how we will buy our school clothes. This is how I will earn those fancy pads of paper I like better than the ones the school provides. This, my father says, is a lesson in economics.

The tractor comes to the end of a row. Tom pulls the picker through the ditch. I lift my legs off the footholds, brace them away from the stinging nettles. For a minute there is the disorientation of facing back the way we came. Then Tom aligns the picker with the rows and we bend again to the picking, leaning down, legs spread, reaching between our knees to break these stalks coming more heavily now with every acre. I wipe sweat from my face, smearing my cheek with asparagus juice and dust. The scent is acidic and sharp. The wind turns dry as we finish the second acre. My jaw aches from clenching my teeth. My hands are slow and my body feels sluggish. The heat fills the field like hot soup in a hot cup.

Out of the corner of my eye, I watch my mother pick the spears and tend Patti's shade blanket in the same motion. I miss stalks. I watch Tom, in the driver's seat, wipe his face by pulling his shirt up, then pull his cap low over his eyes against the sun. I miss more. I watch Rick get up to clean the row ends and fill his bushels faster. Even Marijo shares a row with Marilyn, a neighbor. I wonder if I could die.

"Close to the ground." My father shouts. He has been walking unnoticed behind the picker. His voice is sharp. Every ounce is money. The processor doesn't want white butts, a phrase that provides an endless source of humor for my brothers. But my father wants the weight, not the docking he will get if the white butts show up in the processor's sample, not the reduction of cents per pound if the tips are broken.

We bow our heads to soil as though someone announced prayer. The field is heavy with crop, stalks thick and lush after the rain two days ago. The steady thunk dulls as the crates fill. I glance up. He is looking directly at me.

I miss a stalk, break another too high.

He walks behind my row. I know he is following. I half try to catch the stalks and half don't. At the end of the row, when Tom again makes the turn, he gestures for me to get off the picker. He points to Marijo to take my place.

I stand before him. He holds out his large, capable hands. There, in his broad palms are a half-dozen missed stalks, tips broken from passing under the picker when they should have been picked. There too are a dozen or so butts, two or three inches of weight. How many ounces does he hold? He looks at me. "You can do better than this." It is all he says. He throws the wasted green to the side, turns and heads for his truck to load crates. I stand in the dry heat, the sun blazing against the back of my head.

I look at the sky and close my smarting eyes. Why can't I be like Rick and count my bushels, like Tom in the tractor's seat, like Marijo, trundling along cheerfully? What is wrong with me? What can I do but turn back to the field, something like dirt filling my mouth.

How much later is it that I am riding the picker next to my mother?

How many acres have passed under our hands before, in the rotation of things, I am seated over the row next to hers? Her eyes are as sharp as my father's and I am still stung to the core by his singling me out. But she doesn't say anything. She works, leaning down to the earth. I feel her voice in my head, telling me that the only way to get anywhere is through work, asking do I really want new school clothes. I answer her silence as though she has spoken.

"I'll never have enough money for school clothes," I whine in a voice that I am pretty sure will trigger her don't-feel-sorry-for-yourself response. *Anything,* I think. But it doesn't happen. Her face gets quiet. She makes a decision.

"You may not need to worry about school clothes," she says slowly.

Does this mean I am to wear last years'?

"My dresses are too small," disgust in my voice. She knows this is true. This spring I have had such a growth spurt my bones and muscles ache with it.

She sighs, leans, breaks the stalk perfectly at the surface, tosses it into the crate. "Your father and I are thinking about something else." Snap, then the thunk, a small, irregular drum.

Is this the moment when my heart, like some newly caged bird, comes to settle on its roost? Is it that moment that I come back to my body for the first time in days, come back to the way of our lives? I hear the workers. I hear the Mendoza family speaking their soft Spanish, the warm rhythm of a language I will always associate with fields. I hear my sister Marijo singing her same song as she too leans over her long brown legs to break the green. A killdeer calls sharply over the thrum of the engine.

"We are thinking we could afford to send you to Catholic school this fall."

"Catholic school?" Is it then I lift my head, breathe in the black cream of diesel, the chartreuse odor of fresh cut asparagus, and past that, the whiffs of pine and cool swamp? Is that when the world begins to change again?

"St. Joseph's school. The big parish. We pass it on the way to town. The brick church. If you went there, you would wear a uniform."

I have no words.

She turns to me. Her hands do the necessary work without thought. "It would mean a lot of work. It would depend on the season. On the money. On you." She turns to check her bushel. She calls up to my brother, "We'll need to dump these at the end." She sees possibility balanced in this green, but it is work that works magic. It is the will and the force of their bodies against the heat and play of the field. In that moment, she gives it to me.

I see the school. The story remade, the dream stretching back from its point in the future to touch even the heat of this day. It saves me from the small-heartedness that had been punching its way into my cells. The house that is a field opens again to infinite green; the walls disappear, the world grows large. I bend to it, this work. For the fourth time, I will change one of the houses of my life. Snap, snap.

All the rest of the day I pick close to the ground.

SHIFTING LINES

I want to learn to be good, to learn to pray. I have been told it is hard but possible. But what do I know, the summer before fifth grade, of how the exalted can change you? What do I know of change?

Ours has always been the smaller parish, the mission church to the east of Hart, way out in the sticks. A church nearly Protestant in its simplicity, a church so old there existed both Indian and white people's cemeteries. My mother grew up in that church, the church where her Belgian immigrant father saw that she was baptized, where she married my father. Now, my mother will give up the parish where many of her people are buried, the church where the local Indians, migrants, and friends she grew up with, successful or not, have always attended Mass, made confession. To enroll me in St. Joseph's school, my parents must petition the Diocese to change to St. Joseph's parish in Weare. For once, our remoteness works for us. Located on the far western border of one parish, we become the farm on the far eastern border of the larger parish. A simple shifting of lines.

Our new church is so big that farmers who live in the already sweeping height of timber-framed barns call this church a *cathedral*. It rises, slate-roofed and high-belled, above the corn and wheat and work, above the concerns swirling like dust devils in the frame farmhouses. Its white-trimmed steeple ascends over fields that spread like rugs around it. It becomes, over half a century, gnomon and landmark in the county.

Saint Joseph, we are taught, is patron saint of carpenters, of manual labor, and ordinary work that must be done with our hands. The right saint for people of hard acres, the right name for a country church. But this church is contradictory to the saint's persona, an anomaly ornamented to within an inch of its life. Women who are otherwise unimpressed by trappings enter the oak-carved doors with their plastic purses and fussy kids, lift their faces to the ten-foot windows stained with saints and biblical figures holding the symbols of doctrine and biblical law, and they shush their children. Men with manure on their boots and hard bills on their minds cross into a nave buttressed with columns, peppered with Latinate statues, hung with a Dresden blue, and they lower their heads. They kneel who kneel only for planting. This structure, as much as their obligation to God, calls to the solid hearts of people whose thresholds are worn, whose windows rattle in the wind, who know the heartache of trouble. Thus, the church is also a house of pride as much as spirit. Parents and grandparents raised the money to build it here at the north end of the county so that daughters can be confirmed here, sons married here. If there is no other place they can point to as grand in their lives, they can point to this, their church.

Our church.

Dressed in our clean and pressed best, we park the car in the school lot. We cross the road to the wide doors. We look at each other sideways. Tom checks his zipper. Rick squints up at the steeple. My father wears a tie, my mother a hat. We are quiet as we enter the lobby where a man with thick dark hair hands us the bulletin of the week. My parents nod and greet him. We walk through this narrow lobby, wafting with stale incense, our feet scuffling as we bless ourselves with holy water from the font. We move cautiously into the church. Instead of walking down the

First communion

center aisle where everyone can see us, my mother moves to the side, not to draw too much attention to ourselves. My brothers walk quietly, holding themselves like they had to pee but don't want to tell anyone; my sisters hold my mother's hands. The light spills through translucent windows of Saint Elizabeth, Saint Peter, Paul on the Road to Damascus. We walk through the warm reds, the cool blues of their robes.

We find a pew near my old Aunt Mary's, for this has always been her church. When we have all genuflected and settled, she glances and nods to us. My mother's eyes meet hers. A deeply held look passes between them, her version of welcome.

We kneel. We lift our heads to the castle-esque altar of white marble and gold trim, graced with tall brass candlesticks and secret dust, all of it designed to draw the eye to the tabernacle, the golden door, the cubby lined with shining copper where the Eucharist is housed.

It is my first encounter with the majestic.

The priest enters, vestments shimmering. The altar boys, seventh and eighth graders, carry more candles and the sparkling cruets for the water and the wine. The priest, solemn and rustling, raises his hands, *In nomine patris, et felii, et spiritus sancti.* The sisters' rosaries tap the pews like raindrops. I see my Aunt Mary, her gray eyes attentive in a way I have never seen before. I try to see what she sees.

Candles are lit, though it is daytime.

I try, perhaps for the first time, to speak the prayers, not by rote, not as something to get done. I try, in the face of this church where we belong now, to say the Latin phrases that I know by heart. I try to make the hymns with their beautiful words, *Oh most Holy Trinity, undivided unity,* come to my mouth with purpose, these words of beeswax and incense and tall spires. These words of candles in daytime.

I think of my Aunt Mary and the nuns and the sonorous rhythm of Latin. I want this place where the light falls on our hands and makes them glow. I want my prayers distilled into the sweeping architecture overhead, prayers not just in but of this new house. I shape the words. I follow the spires of the altar up and up toward the kaleidoscope of the high windows. I try and try and still my words do not feel the way I think they should.

How long will it take to learn to pray here?

How long before this loneliness will pass?

AUNT MARY

After my Uncle John died on that fateful Christmas Eve, my Aunt Mary *gave herself to the life of prayer.* That is how it is said. In the years that followed, she prayed with such constancy that it became her signature behavior. And perhaps because of this it is to her that my mother looks when I start at St. Joseph's Catholic School. It is to her that she turns to fulfill the hope that I will find my way back into her world.

When my mother wakes me that first September morning to attend the new school, only the slimmest light spills from the east. In thin pajamas and a plain overcoat, with a paper sack into which I've stuffed my new uniform, I leave our farmhouse, climb into the old Nash, and ride the miles to Weare Township. It is so early I fall asleep in the car. When my father wakes me again with a gentle nudge, I climb out into air so early even the nearby dairy farms have not let the milk cows to pasture. My father's car shifts, its engine blurring away into the weak tea of September light. He will drive on to Montague where he will work all day in the DuPont plant before returning to work the fields for the length of another day that will end long after dark. The price did not hold on one crop or another. This is how he is making it. Farmers all over the county are deciding the same.

I walk up the driveway toward the small brick bungalow bordered by a row of horse chestnut trees on one side and a cornfield on the other. It stands next door to the church. It is where my Great Aunt Mary and Uncle John moved when they sold their farm. It is to this house I am dropped because the one bus that carries parochial school children cannot come all the way to our farm. At its door, in the cool shadows of dawn, I look to the west. The roofline of St. Joseph's Church and the school just now catch the first shock of sunlight. I turn to enter the house where I will wait until my school day begins. The house where, since my Uncle John's death, my Great Aunt Mary lives alone.

This small house is to be the staging area for goodness. She is the saint now. She is the one for whom the rosary and Mass have become her daily work. Of course, we eat her cookies, oatmeal raisin and peanut butter. We watch her stitch the quilts. But we know. We see her lips move, her face turn toward the cross. It is prayer that makes her life. It is to her we assign sainthood. In every parish there is one.

I pull open the side door of her house, climb the rough stairs, and slip into the kitchen that smells of fried eggs and burnt toast and old water. There is the pedestal table in the kitchen, set already with chipped bowls. I tiptoe through an arched opening to the living room where two leather-covered chairs face each other like large sleeping animals near the plain brick fireplace. The leather is cracked and smells heavier than other furniture. It is cold. I pull an afghan from the backrest, curl it around me. Somewhere in the room there still sits the small elegant tobacco cabinet lined with shining copper that holds my dead uncle's pipes, and the basket of spools that are the only toys she provides other than a deck of cards with the jacks missing. Over her chair is also a dark Dutch cuckoo clock that functions perfectly. Other than that, the only ornaments in the room are a cross on the wall and the picture of the Pope.

I stand in the dark, shivering despite the afghan, waiting.

Aunt Mary enters from one of the two small rooms in the back. She is fully dressed, with a sturdy, full-breasted country body, thick ash-colored hair braided and wrapped around her head in a tight crown, a firm mouth, and high cheekbones gone jowly with age. She does not smile. She goes first to the clock, pulls the chain slowly, the sound ratcheting through the dim room. The tick halts, begins again, steadies its strange pulse. It is six thirty. She moves to her chair, looks at the body on the cross, makes the sign of the cross.

"Ready to pray?" she asks. I nod though I wonder if I can stay awake. I hold out my palm for the rosary she gives me, a plastic white one, for I have forgotten my own and she knows this already. She sits in her chair and begins the Apostles Creed, *I believe in one God . . . ,* then what we call the "Our Father," but what I will learn later is the "Lord's Prayer" to the rest of the world. Then on to the Hail Marys in units of ten. *Hail Mary, full of grace . . .* and the response halfway through the prayer, *Holy Mary, mother of God, pray for us sinners. . . .* As the light gathers, her rough voice with its guttural note of Dutch will lead me through the sixty-plus prayers that make up the rosary.

I have prayed the rosary in church and with my family since I was old enough to learn. It is the one time when our voices are in unison, like singing but spoken, regular as the sound of bees. It is safe too, for when many people pray the rosary together no one's voice is too important. Enough people speaking together will cover someone like me, a dreamer, who drops out for a while.

But this is the rosary with one person, the woman the entire community has called a saint because she is the one who prays for everyone, attends Mass every day. She makes novenas for Christmas gifts. She gives money to the sisters and helps with anything the church asks of her. As far as I can tell, her only indulgence is that once a year, on Easter Sunday after Easter Mass, after we have all gone through the long days of Holy Week rituals, she serves a rich Polish sausage breakfast for our entire family.

I want to pray with her, am willing to say an entire rosary before I dress for school, before I carefully cross the country road, turn back, wave to her shadow, and enter the world of the Dominican sisters who will be my teachers.

From her, I will learn to be good at last.

But there is a secret I think about sometimes when I enter the house that is now hers alone. In the church next door, my Uncle John died. The church where I will go now. She was present for his death. What I imagine there at the back of the church before the last rites and the slow ambulance and the undertakers and the steel-gray coffin is her face, her eyes watching his in those last moments when he saw the lights changing. And in my heart I wonder: is it the thing in his eyes that makes her pray? Or the thing in her own eyes she saw in his? Is it the scene I have conjured that made an ordinary widow into the one we turn to for our goodness? Or is there something to this invented moment? What is it in all their faces, in the face of so many of our home-grown deaths, that makes this one so exceptional, that says we must pray so hard that we can become what we are not?

THE SCHOOL

The most important word I learn that first day is *present*.

Across the street from the church, its practical mate. In yellow brick, the two-story square building that is St. Joseph's Catholic School is better named than the church. It rises to face the church, hip-roofed and green-guttered, blockier, brighter, more practically made. Where the church faces south to the summer sun, the school faces north to the cool even light of a practicality that enhances the church's beauty rather than balances it. It is sturdy. It is safe. Look, there is a fire escape. Its iron-grated treads hold such a sense of oddity and security that students beg for fire drills. Look, here are the small solid doors, thrown open like arms each morning, caught with ordinary eye hooks. Look inside, the center hall-way and staircase is varnished to a dark mirror but sheaves of light spill in from the classrooms on the east side, or from the sisters' residence on the west, creating in the play of light the high contrasts that will be our lives.

The school is partly like the one-room schools, partly like the many-roomed consolidated schools. Here are two classrooms, one for first through fourth grades, one for fifth through eighth grades. Solid yellow walls are punctuated with wide, high windows with a smaller window above, called a transom, for more light and air. The ceilings rise to ten feet, and fans, two with dark wings, spin the air. East light, with its particular clarity, spills into the classrooms all morning long, then evens into comfortable cooler shadow through the afternoon. Here, everything is clean and old. This world is so established it demands attention; it must be respected.

Its most significant characteristics are tall black-and-white angels in the flowing habits of the Marywood Dominicans. They are the teachers we have been told they will be: disciplined and energetic, smart and well-educated. They will lead the children of farmers out of the backyards of ignorance while at the same time ensuring they remain faithful Catholics. Theirs is a school of order and the beauty of the well-taught lesson, of rules so strict they squeak, coupled with the almost addictive excitement called learning.

This couple, church and school, face each other in comfortable superiority. They are long-married, capable, loyal, complementary leaders of a small country.

I climb the stoop of the brick schoolhouse, walk through the mudroom, through the room called a foyer, into the hallway, up the stairs to the second-floor classroom. Sister stands at the top of the stairs and watches as I take off my coat and hang it on the row of hooks. She is dressed in a white habit with a black veil. She wears black shoes with hard heels and on the highly polished wooden floors, these heels make a drum of clear swiftness, and that sound, hers or any of the sisters' footsteps on the stairs, in the hall, in the classroom, is linked to the patter of her beads, the soft clicking of the long rosary, the fifteen-decade rosary looped to her belts, a rosary it is whispered they pray every day.

Sister settles us into our seats with the ringing of a brass bell that has a bright clear sound like not quite ripe grapes. She lifts her hands, we stand next to our seats. She leads the prayers I have yet to learn, the

Angelus, the *Confiteor.* She tells us about the gospel for the day, the one about the Angel Gabriel who was the first to say the *Hail Mary.* She tells us that while she is taking attendance, we should think about the gospel. Then she does something I have never seen a teacher do. She calls each of our names, and as she does, she looks at us directly, all forty of us. A name and a look. And when she looks at a child, that child answers clear and plain, *present.* Is it a gift? Are we to have a present for someone, or to give a present? There is nothing on our desks, no packages. When she comes to me, she looks at me and stops.

"Anne-Marie Oomen?" She says my whole name. For a moment I am so startled and pleased I cannot speak.

She waits.

"What is it, child?"

"Why do we say present?"

Although there is tittering in the room, she is not unkind.

"It means you are here."

I am here. I look around the bright room, the heads bent or watchful, the uniforms of crisp blue plaid, the texture of our bodies in rows, even the gleaming floors. The light spills in and I hold this new meaning to me, whole and unchecked—the gift of being here.

ON BECOMING A SAINT

The church is beautiful, the music haunting, the lessons full of new words, and Aunt Mary is my watchful guide in this school where every day is like a good day fishing. We carry rosaries and *textbooks*. The priest teaches us the *biblical interpretation* and we learn science from "Mr. Science" on TV. The sisters float over our lives like benevolent clouds.

Still it doesn't take me many weeks to realize that this school moves in a wheel of repetition, a familiar itch that makes me pick at the last-of-season mosquito scabs until they bleed. At first I don't know why my mind strays to the leaf-laden playground, the bookcases, or even back home where my sisters and brothers are going to my old school. What makes me dream of the weedy, demanding fields of my home when I have the broader fields of this place?

Stones in a field. The old ways rise. Mornings get harder, days longer, the Masses methodical. Here it does not matter that I am a good reader because there is new math, physical science, and history with a list of dates back to the Egyptians. It is not easy. I learn the names of prophets but forget the names of Greek columns. I learn fractions, but fail the test where we must write the long numbers as they are spoken aloud. I listen less to the sisters' voices and more and more to their sharp footsteps.

I sit in a desk two rows over from the bookshelves. Between classes I stare longingly, wishing I could bury myself in any book that would not end with Noah, Elijah, or the Pope's blessing. After Bryan, the Irish boy with a million freckles, has humiliated me in a catechism quiz, I stare at the books so I don't have to look at anyone else. My eyes meander from encyclopedias to hymnbooks. Nothing. What finally swims into my vision is a series of red books with tattered but similar bindings. They are stacked at the bottom of the farthest shelf. I think maybe they are a series, like Nancy Drew or the Hardy Boys, or even Spin and Marty, my new favorite, but if that were the case, they would be checked out. Why aren't these books checked out?

I ask to be excused. On the way back from the bathroom I squat next to the bookcase to tie the shoe I untied in the bathroom. I lean over and slip the book out of its slot and carry it under my vest back to my desk. *The Life of Saint Lucy.* My sigh is deep and long, but I flip it open. The flyleaf reads, "gave herself to Jesus and chose death rather than lose the incorruptible treasure of her virginity." *Incorruptible treasure of her virginity.* What does virginity mean? I look it up in the big dictionary, trying not to blush as I figure it out.

Wow!

She chose death instead of . . . I flip for the phrase, *being defiled.* I turn to page one. And here is my little salvation, a story laced with melodrama but legitimate enough that the nuns will forgive me. I look back to the bookshelf and count. There are at least two dozen volumes of *Lives of the Saints.* At recess I check out *St. Lucy.* The next day, I check out three more. After that, I just take them.

One evening, after finding two volumes of *Lives of the Saints* in my unmade bed and one stuffed in a lunch box that never got properly emptied, my mother asks, not without some irritation, "Who this time?"

Was it Linus? Or Teresa? Jerome? The names roll in my mouth like candy. I check. Today, "Saints Cyprian and Justina."

"And just who were they?" I miss the pointy sound in her question.

I clear my throat, enjoying the retelling. "Cyprian was a magician, and he tried to get Justina to join him in sorcery but she's so good she finally convinces him to join her, but then . . ." I turn a page or two and drift off. Someone yells *Rifleman.* My siblings abandon the table for the TV, but the Rifleman cannot hold a candle to the acts of the martyred saints.

I look up with delight, "They both get beheaded." I bury my nose in the book, ignoring the dishes piled around me that I should be clearing off the table. My mother slams a pot in that universal language that people more aware than I would recognize. My father looks up from the last of his fried potatoes, quietly observing my mother and me. "Never know about beheadings. Could happen right here."

In these books, there is always the noble, brave, and victorious saint. There is always some great evil to be fought, some heroic act to be carried out—leading the early Christians out of the catacombs, arguing with the civil authorities—there is always that evil magistrate, battling the Romans, pagans, Goths (*What's a Goth, Sister?*), and then there are the horrible ways a saint can die, being torn apart by animals; or having your breasts cut off, your eyes poked out, and being fed to snakes; or being burned at the stake; or my favorite—St. Peter's personal choice—being crucified upside down.

Of course, *God gives special powers to the truly faithful so they won't feel pain,* I tell my mother. She stirs the soup so hard it splashes over the side of the pan.

I decide I want to be a saint.

It must be simple I think, must be something amazing and clear and one just does it, doesn't one?

But there is the problem I have with every day. Every day, I run when I am supposed to walk, complain when I am supposed to be compliant, argue when I am supposed to agree. I am not a saint. I am not even very good.

But if I could go to a Saint School, maybe . . . I try it out on Sister.

"How do regular people become saints?" I ask her quietly, not wanting to let on my plans too soon.

She looks at me over her glasses, "You can start by being a good Catholic."

There is no such thing as Saint School?

And being a good Catholic doesn't look anything like being a saint. Why these quiet prayers rather than sword fighting like Joan of Arc? Where is the devil, or even just an ordinary bad guy, who I can battle? But the sisters tell me that the devil is in the daily battles, that saintliness lies in being patient with our little brothers and sisters, in being kind to people who have less than we do, in doing our lessons and chores and saying our prayers. Like my Aunt Mary. They point out that there are saints who did nothing but pray their whole lives.

I skip those.

My favorite is Saint Rose of Lima, the girl who laughed at Satan. The first Saint from this side of the planet, she was feeble and weak, but she stood up to Satan, laughed right in his face, even though he showed her every temptation and evil vision in his bag of tricks. *She laughed at him.* Oh, just give me the chance for that kind of bravery.

But instead, I say the rosary with Aunt Mary. I go to Mass and learn the prayers. In class I learn the names of the planets and their distances from the sun and their regular rotations and orbits. But I cannot stop the days' regular march. I wiggle in my chair. Sister has to come, put her hand on my shoulder, and not say a word until I can take out my books. But under every fact about Mars, I want to know what will make me a saint.

It is morning again and I am fumbling for my clothes in the small cold bathroom of Aunt Mary's house. The weather is so bitter it is like a cold smoke filling every space. The car never warmed as we drove the long miles from the farm to her house. I never fell back to sleep for the precious half hour, one of the reasons I remain in pajamas until I get to her house. So I am tired; my uniform is cold, the towels are cold, the rug feels damp, the water never gets hot. Teeth trembling, I pull off my pajama top, pull out the tee shirt, the blouse, and shrug them on. I step out of the pajama bottoms and reach for my underwear. My hands come up empty. I cannot find the plain cotton panties from J. C. Penney's that are the only ones my mother will let me wear though I asked for the ones with lollipops. I shiver in the cold, turn the sack upside down. The plaid skirt and slip fall out. A pair of socks falls out.

No panties. My upper lip dampens with sweat, my face burns despite the chill. I wrap the towel around me. I trundle into the living room where Aunt Mary is working a quilt on a fir frame.

"Can I call my mom?"

Aunt Mary looks up from the quilting frame. "What's the matter?"

I can't tell her out loud. I move through the dim light to the tiny desk in the living room. I pick up the handset of the black rotary phone and spin the number. My mother answers immediately but I know from the grumbling and squalling in the background that she is getting the boys ready for the bus and the little girls are awake. "Mom, I forgot my panties."

Aunt Mary snorts.

"Can you bring them, Mom? Mom?"

I can hear a breathy sigh that is an answer. "You know your Dad has the car."

"Borrow Uncle Butler's car."

"He's working too."

She pauses, says the unthinkable. "You could go without."

"Mom, I can't go to school without panties. I can't." Her suggestion is so unbearable to me that I think she must be nuts.

Is that when I start to cry?

"Let me talk to Aunt Mary," she says.

I hand the phone to my aunt who has limped away from the quilting frame. I remember that she and Uncle John were strict with us in ways that my mother explains by saying, *They never had any children.*

Will she help?

When she places the phone in its black cradle, her face is set like a rock. She walks into her bedroom. I trail slowly. She rummages through her drawers until she finds a pair of her own. Her gnarled hands place them in my cold ones. I run to the bathroom and pull them on but the minute I let go of the elastic, the panties drop.

"Do they fit?" she calls from the hallway.

"The legs are by my knees." But I am desperate. "Do you have safety pins?"

"Yah. I get them."

But even with safety pins, it is like wearing a tent with holes for legs. I am trying not to sob. She sits on the edge of her bed and folds her hands and prays for a moment. Then she looks up. "We will make you something."

"What?'

"A diaper."

"A diaper? I can't wear a diaper." What does she know about diapers?

With growing dread I follow her to the kitchen where she takes a stack of clean soft rags out from under the kitchen counter. She finds one that she holds to my waist. She gives me two safety pins.

"Here, pin the corners at the top on the two sides, like this, and make them snug, then put on your skirt."

"How will I pee?"

"You'll have to take the pins out."

"What if someone sees?"

"Don't drop it and they won't see."

"Do you have more pins?"

"No."

I stumble into the bathroom and rig the diaper as she has suggested, though with every move, my face becomes a fever. The top of the diaper bunches at my waistband and feels thick as a wheel. It bunches between my legs. I pull the skirt over it. It puffs at the top and makes a roll, then falls to an almost normal length. I can't keep from feeling it, the dense clump of cloth riding on top of my hips, the pull between my legs. It is all wrong. I feel a rocketing panic. I cannot go to school in a diaper. "Aunt Mary, it doesn't work," I insist as I show her.

She looks at me, bends, pulls at the skirt hem, evening it out. "Looks fine. Wipe your nose and come for breakfast."

I am to go forward whether I like it or not. I stand at the table instead of sitting so nothing will change position. I slip my hand under my skirt and try to tuck the top under my waistband for extra security.

"Don't do that." She frowns.

"What if it falls off?"

"The pins are tight?"

"I don't know."

"Ach, eat your oatmeal." She lifts her cup. Her face will not budge. I do as I am told, dreading the day as it lightens to its November shape. I finish my cereal and carry the bowl to the sink. I look at her face. No sympathy.

"Offer it up." She says.

"Offer it up?"

"Offer up the discomfort to God for your sins of forgetfulness. You will remember next time."

I walk slowly across the street to my school, nauseous with worry, trying to think about this offering up. I am to offer up to God my embarrassment for having to wear a diaper because I forgot my panties? But I try. During morning prayers, standing at the side of our desks, led by the sisters, I try to explain to God what happened. I tell God that I will offer up this diaper, this *wad of fabric* for my sins. But when I think of what I know of God, I can't help but feel doubtful. His discussions with Saint Lucy and Saint Rose don't cover diapers. There is no bravery here, only nervous dampness.

I go to the lavatory to check. I pin and unpin and try to pin tighter, but somehow the fabric slips and always feels loose. I try to catch the top and press it under the waistband to make it secure but it never stays and within minutes I am anxious again, feeling at my waist to see if the pins have come undone. What if they stick me? What if I bleed and die? My love for the brave deaths of the saints squirms away; I discover I don't want to die and bravery becomes a mystery. I sit very still in my seat. I sit through math and reading lessons. After awhile, I think that if I don't move again all day long, I might make it through this.

But then the bright room fills with the church bell's long tones. Ten fifteen on Wednesday. This is the day for mid-morning Mass. This is the day we get out of our seats, stand in line, march down the stairs, out the doors, across the street, and into church for daily Mass where we will kneel and stand and rise and kneel again according to the rites.

I rise with the others. I move slowly, trying to keep my knees together, trying to keep everything in place. I manage my coat. I manage the stairs. But it's hard to walk with your knees together. It's slow. Halfway across the street, Maryann bumps into me and looks at me like she knows. When I genuflect, I don't bless myself but keep my hands tightly clasped, pressed against my tummy so that nothing shifts. I stand carefully and sit by sliding backward on the seat. Once, while kneeling, I lift my skirt, slide my hand under, and try to adjust the thing. One of the big girls turns sideways to look at me. I flush, letting the skirt drop. They all know. There is nothing, absolutely nothing, in that church but their eyes. I tell myself to muster bravery, the courage to fight a lion.

It doesn't work for a diaper.

I look up at the majestic altar, at the pinnacles and the high blue ceiling, and wonder how this can be happening. I was going to be a saint with long robes, one of those in the rich red or light blue, one who would lead in the face of any threat, who would die for my faith. But here I am, wearing a diaper to Mass because I forgot my underwear. I look around at all the saints in the glass windows and all of the statues and Stations of the Cross and the vested priest and the calm nuns, and finally at my Aunt Mary, not smiling today, not even looking at me. I know that I am not a saintly person, that I will never fight Satan, never die a martyr.

I am the kind of person who loses her panties.

I look at the light, bend my head, breathe a true prayer, "Oh, Lord, have mercy on me."

SECOND SCAR

The second scar is about winter, about plain clumsiness, about our family locked for too long in that remote farmhouse during a snowstorm. It is about wounds and death. Here is evening at the end of a day marked by drafts and frost-ridden windows and bickering. There are toys and unfinished games scattered throughout the living room. There are arguments about Lincoln Logs and BB guns and how loud the television can be. Outside, blizzard conditions.

Up the north road, in another farmhouse, Uncle Butler is dying.

Three or four times a day my mother drives or walks the quarter mile to their place. It is because she worked as a nurse during the war. Aunt Evelyn has asked; the doctor has said yes. He trusts my mother. He provides syringes, something called morphine. It is a winter full of secrets that I know are there only because of the way they smell.

My mother is what my father calls bone tired, but the words mix up in my head and I think the phrase is stone tired. As the days pass, I watch her come home after each visit up the road. I can see her face is not thinking about us, still as a stone with some knowledge too hard to talk about.

Once or twice I go with her. I watch as she rubs the thin skin of the man I no longer recognize, who is wizened and silent, whose bed now inhabits the dining room so it is close to the kitchen, close to warmth and water. In that room, conversation is so low and broken it is like a machine that will not restart, the starter grinding down to nothing. It is there I get close to the secret, that smell of old urine, cigarette smoke, something of the body when it cannot heal. Animals when they are dying. A dog, just before he goes to the woods to dig the last quiet hole under a log, smells the way a man smells in a close room, letting go of days. After a while I don't go anymore. None of us goes, even my father when he is home.

She goes alone.

It is early evening, dark, on one of those days. I am running down the staircase, the wide and open stairs we have been forbidden to run down. My arms are loose with motion, up and out. I am flying down into the living room, that space of toys and irritation, when—how does this happen—balance leaves me. Did I slip on the rod of a Tinkertoy, the random tee shirt waiting to be carried up? It may have been me, again misjudging distance, the way things—bodies—move through space.

The room shifts, teeters, tips toward the floor. There is a split second of free fall where pictures, wallpaper, newel post blur with speed, then a whir of air in the lungs, the floor rising fast and hard and stupid. The fall ends there. On my hands and knees. The shock ripples down my back. The heels of my hands jar with impact against a crumpled rug that prevents the skin from breaking. But at the bottom of that stairway is a heating duct, a square of ornate iron stamped with swirls of nineteenth-century filigree. My knees strike the duct. The left kneecap takes on the pattern of iron like an old-fashioned and complicated cookie cutter.

How many times in my life does my mother come running? This time it is not at my scream but because of the screams of my little sisters, because my brothers are shouting that it is not their fault. There I am, holding my legs in the kind of pain that has no scream.

"She just fell." Tom says with a half shrug. He does not understand this, how one can just fall. It would not happen to him.

She comes, lifts, looks, touches this wound, ragged to the bone. She knows it is the kind of cut that should have stitches. She looks at the clock, the dark outside. She looks at the snow rushing past the living room window in ragged clots. She knows the thing called morphine will last but an hour more, will be needed again a few hours later. She can barely see the yard light. Snow and more snow. Her daughter should go to the hospital for stitches. Her old friend and neighbor is dying. Can she make it to town and back in time? In this weather? If she makes it, would she be stuck for the night? I see on her face a storm that I will not understand for many years.

Then it resolves.

She is brisk and efficient. She knows what to do. I am not brave but she is patient with my whimpering. She washes, presses, and douses with iodine, which is when pain hits for real. She butterflies the torn flesh, soothes me. "No harm done," she whispers. She touches me gently. By the time I am calm and appeased with ice cream, she needs to leave again.

I see it as she shuts the door and moves out into the cold. Stone tired.

When—is it days or weeks later—he dies in the old dining room, the air in our small world shifts, turns teary and warm. But with it, a deep breath and my mother sleeps for an entire night. It is the quiet rest that comes after long effort. Then she returns to us, our squirrelly bodies, our small dramas. That simple.

Against her best home care, the cut never heals correctly. The scar tissue gathers, defiant to order, puckers in dark pink clumps, is tender to the touch. It rises, a rough and ornery fault line over my kneecap, something she touches with a short sigh. She calls it "proud flesh" a phrase they use for horse wounds. Months later our doctor freezes the area around the knee, cuts away the thick scar, pulls the good skin together to make a line that is clean and straight, though it retains a touch of the redness, a wideness like a mouth. Because I am young and healthy, this new scar heals and fades, becomes another whispered word, one that teaches what is important.

COLOR WHEEL

For the third time, Sister teaches the color wheel. This time, she gives us shiny new compasses that are not like the ones my father uses in the woods but are something altogether different; these make a perfect circle. We are applying a math lesson, a small lesson in geometry, to our art lesson. We are to make a circular design, like a clock, or like a little kid's flower but with perfect petals. The petals must number twelve to show primary, secondary, and tertiary colors. Like the twelve apostles, she reminds us, drawing a parallel I am tired of.

The room is quiet with concentration. I am at my desk with the shiny new compass. I am trying to turn it steadily as she has shown us, but there is now a hole at the center of my paper. When I lift it, I have pushed through the cardboard protector underneath. There is a tiny puncture in the surface of the desk. I try to rub it out, to start again. But I can't hold the compass steady on its point and pivot it in its perfect circle unless I push down. I push too hard. Another tiny dent.

Sister stops next to my desk. She takes the compass, placing my hand around it and her hand around mine. With her hand guiding, we make the arcs until I have something like three petals to a flower. She tells me, "Twelve, four, and eight o'clock." That's how you know where the first three petals, the primary colors, should go. Then she tells me to repeat the pattern, to insert petals in between the ones I have. I push too hard, the compass slips, and this time the paper tears. She sighs the way my mother does when my brothers have tracked in manure. We start again. I manage to remember how to space the petals evenly, but then I insert four petals between eight and twelve instead of three. I start again. I turn the compass; I make the arcs. I am thinking there should be motion in something called a wheel, but the color wheel does not move or roll or leave tracks of any kind. Nothing about it moves except the short pencil around its spearlike pivot.

Once I get the petals right, I put the colors in. The sisters teach us to do this with just five colors, three primaries plus black and white. Cindy Grace paints a perfect wheel by mixing primary colors to make secondary colors. Then, inside the petals, she makes smaller petals that actually get lighter toward the center because she mixes in white for a *tint. Geesh!* Her wheel is like a window in the church, like a flower with every petal the same shape but in different ranges of colors.

I sit at my desk. Do blue and yellow really make green? Is that possible? If so, then what makes purple? And if I get mixed up when I start to put the colors in the wheel and have to remix, they all just turn black. Sister tells me there are tones of black; she suggests I observe this phenomenon. I do for about one minute, but the color mixing is boring.

Sister stands behind me like a cloud pressing down. "Don't dawdle, child." Her voice is firm. *Don't dawdle.* But I can't seem to do what I am supposed to. Long minutes pass and the class finishes their stiff paper wheels. Brushes are rinsed, jars are washed, and paints capped, but I am not caught up. I pick up the compass and press the point into my palm hard enough to make a pink mark, which I like.

The new art teacher is not tall or slim or pretty, but I have never seen anyone who looks like her. She wears full, bright skirts, shawls, and loose sweaters around her full body. She does not wear saddle shoes or the dark shoes of the nuns, but sandals or frayed tennis shoes in faded colors. Her hair is fine, reddish brown with a touch of gray, tucked into a bun or pigtails, even though she is a grown-up. She has freckles. She speaks differently than anyone else I have ever known.

She enters the pine-paneled basement classroom like a queen. She walks from the back to the front, talking all the while. She carries pictures of paintings in a brown folder she calls a portfolio. The prints, as she calls them, are copies of famous paintings from other countries, paintings made in France and Italy, where the Vatican is, she tells us, and even Russia where the communists are. She has studied Art. I have no idea what that means, but I am thinking of the sisters' art classes. My hand rises slowly and I ask, "Will we have to do the color wheel?"

"The color wheel?" she asks. She shakes her head, and her warm-colored hair catches the light from the high windows. "No. Just color."

"Just color?" This from Francis, who wears an expression like a bull on his face. He doesn't want to learn any more about color than I do.

She seems impatient. She answers as though he has asked a different question. "What colors are, how they work, what makes them pure or impure. But not the wheel. You've done that to death."

Done that to death?

"What are we going to do?" Cindy Grace wants to know. She got an A on her color wheel.

"Beauty."

There is a murmur like new water through the class.

Isadora Smith comes to teach art so that the sisters may have preparation time. She teaches three times a week to the little kids and twice to the big kids. She teaches in a way that feels like a ride at the fair.

She sets aluminum *cylinders* and *spheres* (I love these words) on pieces of shiny cloth she calls sateen. She asks us to draw the core shapes because these are at the center of all shapes. I try to draw her sphere, but my lines are uneven, nothing like the straight line the compass makes. She laughs, tells me those are *great potatoes* I have drawn. She says it's okay to make an imperfect shape. She brings wild things from the woods, birds' nests and shelf fungus and mushrooms. We try to find the core shape in the object, until one day I see the sphere in the wrinkled apples, the cone in the last carrots of the year.

She talks about color as if it were a friend. She claims color is warm or cool or crisp or sharp or hot or loud or even tacky. I am skeptical but I want her to like me, for she is not like anyone else I have ever known. She spreads plastic on the floor. She tapes prints to the walls and then blank sheets next to them. She passes out big men's shirts, which we put on backward. Smocks, she calls them. She turns to the table where a dozen different jars of paint and styles of brushes line up on newspaper. She tells us to paint, not the painting itself but what the painting makes us feel; our painting will grow from the painting we pick. We get to choose whichever one is right for us and *just paint*. She never once tells us about four, eight, and twelve o'clock.

The sisters must have plenty of preparation time, because soon there is a new class, called Sexual Education. There has been big talk about this, with meetings at night where people shouted at one another. My mother and father have stood up for it, and our priest has stood up to the school board and has said we will have it. So we have learned some things about our bodies, though it all seems unbelievable to me.

At recess, we go outside because the sisters say we need the air, but we really need to talk about this new thing. The light is gray and the fields spread out, interrupted here and there by piles of plowed snow clotted with mud. The boys play the fox game; they pack down a circle in the snow where they chase the boy who is the fox through this "wheel." They run in their circles, moving, moving, and I wonder if everything is a turning wheel.

Mary Kate, Jenny, and I sit on the bottom steps of the fire escape. Mary Kate is breaking off icicles and sucking them even though we have been told not to do this because they are *unclean*. She doesn't care. We are talking about where babies come from. I tell them what my mother has told me about the egg and sperm. Mary Kate says *we've all heard that,* but she wants to know how it's done, I mean, *exactly* how it is done.

"Well, the sperm penetrates the egg," I say, repeating the words that have been said so carefully to me.

"And just how the hell does that happen?" Mary Kate asks. No one in my family swears, but Mary Kate swears like this a lot and when she does, it makes me feel crazy inside.

Jenny says, "My mom and dad say it happens in bed."

"What the hell is *penetrate* anyway?" Mary Kate again. Jenny looks at her. Two *hells* in one conversation are too much for her. She sounds exactly like a mother when she says, "I don't think this is our business yet."

"Okay, okay, but I don't get it." Mary Kate waves her icicle and matches Jenny's adult voice perfectly. "I think we don't have the whole story here."

They look to me. I don't want to appear stupid about one more thing. I say, making it up, "I think someone has to push something." As I say this I am realizing it seems true. There is something to this pushing that makes the baby. I am sure of it. But it eludes us. None of the pictures in the films make sense. The man and the woman stand next to each other, and though you can see all the parts of the body, they never touch. Separate. They are never shown kissing, which I am sure has to do with this fuss.

The fire escape feels cold on the backs of my legs, even through my leggings, but I feel warm and strange inside. The cloudy light fills the field with shorter distances; the boys run, shouting in pack form, inside their wheel. The golden bell rings and Mary Kate drops her icicle, brushes down her skirt, and says, "Well, I hope we can get to the bottom of this some day."

I want to know now. What is it they will not say in all these classes that are supposed to prepare us for . . . being adults? I want to know why even just talking about it feels strange and warm, yet not all right. Why are they talking about some things and shushing others? Even my mother, who wanted these classes, who has told me carefully about how my periods will happen, hurries on to the next thing when I ask her the man and woman part.

Mrs. Smith teaches watercolor. In that basement classroom where the
light comes down from the high windows and there is no distraction of
weather or fields, she gives us special paper and shows us how to dampen
just the top half. Water poured on paper deliberately, not as a spill, but
something you want, in the middle of the afternoon in a classroom that is
winter dry—it is like a present. I run my fingers over the wet paper, letting the damp drift onto my skin. She shows us how to fill a brush with
color. She tells us to let the color run down the brush to its tip, to let it
gather there, a drop of deep blue. It trembles, lets go, hits the wet paper.
I watch the color spread out in a rough circle, larger and larger. She says,
"Brush it open." Oh. There. Sky. A wash of sky opening on wet paper. A
sudden rush of small breaths around the room: *Look, oh look at mine.*

We keep going. A wash of paler blue, a dark purple. The world is
made of shapes waiting to be unlocked by color, water, and your brush.
She lets us practice making skies until the rinse water turns muddy and
the sisters ring the bell.

But I stay. I like the way the colors fill the wet paper, the way the
paper takes color inside itself. I watch my sky spread up and down on
the sheet like the northern lights. I take another sheet, wet the paper, and
drop blue on one side, yellow on the other. I watch them widen. Blur.
Where they overlap, it happens. Yellow and blue make green.

"Ah, an expressionist."

I jump. She stands next to me. She leans over to study what I have
done. Her body smells of toothpaste and something I cannot identify,
then realize it is tobacco.

"Expressionist?"

"An artist who expresses the idea of the thing instead of the thing
itself. Usually there are strong lines, like this." She picks up a fine brush,
dips it into thick black paint, and deftly outlines all three blobs of color,
making three irregular circles of color. "Now what does it look like?"

"A coloring book."

She laughs out loud, a throaty laugh like none I have ever heard
before. I feel good to have made her laugh. Her head dips toward the
paper as she studies what I have done, which under her gaze looks sillier

and sillier. "Well, I guess so," she says as she straightens up and looks at me. "But now it is something divided from itself, a separation in the world." I look again at the painting. I don't understand how this black line does any more than stop the color, but I want to. I can feel myself reaching for the sentence she has said. *Something divided from itself.*

"I don't get it."

She pauses. "Not yet."

But after that she pays more attention to me and, though it is clear she prefers natural landscapes, she brings in pictures of what she calls Modern Art for us to look at. I look at them, studying their strange shapes. I feel myself pulled toward some sense of meaning that is there and is not there. And I want her to like me. My mother works too hard, Aunt Mary prays too much, the sisters are distant and strict. Maybe she is a grown-up woman who will like me.

I take to announcing the titles of every painting she shows us to whoever will listen. I make a big deal out of knowing the artist's name. I learn that some colors have names that run alive in the mouth, *ochre* and *cadmium.*

"This must be *cerulean blue,*" I say of the Virgin's robe from the era, the Enlightenment. I read notes about the painting. Bryan rolls his eyes when I say this, but Mrs. Smith nods.

Each day that she comes to teach, I listen for the van that has no muffler so that I can help her carry in her boxes and her portfolios, and even some of her own delicate watercolors.

Once again, I am in love.

However, when I speak of Modern Art around our table at home, silence follows. My mother likes Mrs. Smith, knows her from church, but as she wipes down our kitchen table, she says she'd rather see trees in a picture. But she can see I'm interested, so she lets it be.

In contrast, and with old-country distrust, Aunt Mary is sure it is a problem. "They don't look like much to me," she says when I show her. "They've got color but anybody can do that, that mess. No shape at all." I try to explain the shapes, but since I don't understand completely myself, she frowns me to silence. I eat my oatmeal.

Mrs. Smith tells me that what is important is behind the shape.

It is my turn to clean the basement classroom where we have the art classes. I move through the gray light streaming from the high windows. Overhead, footsteps thud through the first-floor classroom letting out for the day. I can distinguish Sister's quick steps, moving back and forth as she picks up and straightens the day of wet wool and lesson books. I sweep the cool linoleum tiles, listening to the bristles against squares the color of dirty dishwater. The room is lonely without my classmates, without Mrs. Smith to warm the drab space. And there is something else, something about the way my body feels that is all wrong. It has been like this for days, one moment like broken glass, the next like heavy fog.

I sweep but stop to look at the tacked-up paintings. I like the ones she calls Impressionist, the soft and lovely colors that seem melted. They make me miss summer. Monet. I come to the ones of the old man holding the blue guitar with his head bent over as if he is being poured into his guitar. There is another of a family standing on the beach, not talking to one another. Divided from themselves. Picasso.

Her portfolio rests on the big table she uses instead of a desk. It is full of prints, perhaps for the next lesson. I stack papers, staring at the portfolio. I pull the trash can out from under the table. When I straighten up, I notice a corner slipping from the edge of the portfolio, a lush rose, part of a larger picture. The color pulls me. I lift the portfolio cover to straighten the print. A man and woman rest on couches covered with brocade. Heavy curtains drape behind them. They are not wearing any clothes. They are embracing. Everything in the picture is rose and orange, warm like the inside of a fire, except around the outside where all the colors get cool and shadowy. I pick it up, peer closely. *Hercules and Omphale?* I look at the way the woman holds the man, the way his body is with hers, how their arms and legs and bare parts tangle with each other. I see it, how they are all connected. I breathe deeply, trying to take it in.

They are not divided.

When I look up, she is at the doorway, her bun loose, its reddish cast warm in the light. I drop the print. It falls with a slippery sound onto the pile. I put my hands behind my back. Above us, Sister's footsteps drum through the ceiling. Mrs. Smith walks to her table, looks down at the painting. The color comes into my face and I know I will cry. I know better. I know we are not ever to look at pictures of naked people. I will be told how bad I am. She picks up the painting. I wait to be scolded and sent away.

When she speaks, her voice sounds like she is praying, "Beautiful, isn't it?"

Beauty? My blush fades under my collar.

We stand together a long time and talk about this man and woman who have such color in their skin, about the light around their play. She tells me about how the artist worked, about the era of the piece, about the pleasure in the lines. I notice the pearls on the woman's neck and tell her they have the colors of the sea.

Imagine the brink of grace, the small knowings a girl has about the body, its beauty and its ways, but which are so inarticulate that there is no way to language yet, but still, still beauty can come, with its pleasure and momentum, and it can be held out to you so that for just a moment you can study it, you can know the world undivided.

UNBRAIDED

Winter in our rural world stretches out in barns, farmhouses, fields, and in our bodies, which become taut with the burden of coats and darkness. Weather wraps us in a cold hand, the harsh cloudiness that closes in on the Great Lakes north. Lake effect rolls across from Wisconsin, storms ride currents down from Canada. When the lake finally freezes, nothing remains to temper the cold. It enters our homes and bones and sits. Today the wind flings snow pellets like small pebbles across the fields, stinging our faces.

An Alberta Clipper.

I struggle with mittens and boots and lost things. I shudder in the chilly classrooms of St. Joseph's. Within its brick walls, I still read the Lives of the Saints, but I am less likely to make sense of their sacrifice. I have begun to wonder about their souls. My soul. Does it think about the world? I have been told there is nothing like heaven, the soul is absolutely happy at last, but I wonder if heaven is all it's cracked up to be. Won't my soul miss the world? Wouldn't a soul miss the feel of flannel, the taste of apple? What do they look like really, these souls that have no shape? When I ask questions, I get no satisfactory answers.

Aunt Mary's brick house never feels warm. In every room I enter, drafts like invisible birds slip under doors, through glass, sinking their talons into me. The morning rosary no longer holds the warm hope it first did. She starts the prayers, *I believe in one God . . .* but I fall asleep in her stiff chair, answering to the god of my body and its boredom.

One day after school I walk back to her house to wait for my father to pick me up on his way home. The cuckoo clock ticks the hours by and he does not come. Finally, my mother calls: Dad will sleep in town tonight so he can get back to work in the morning. She tells me to stay the night with Aunt Mary, to rinse out my socks and underwear for school tomorrow.

Stay with Aunt Mary? I try to say that I need to come home, need to be with the bickering boys, toddling little sisters, Tinkertoys on the floor. Hot soup on the stove. I want to be in the place where if the rooms are not warm the people are warm with rushes of need and trial, and there is always the lovely impatient noise of family. But when I look out the window, the silhouette of the school across the street is nearly blotted out.

I know too much about this weather.

After supper, after homework, after the second rosary of the day, Aunt Mary works a quilt. She clears her throat as she pushes the needle through the scraps of fabric and draws the thread. Each scrap is a part of an old dress or shirt, many from my own family, some from the church handouts, too tattered for reuse. She uses cast-off fabric, and rarely buys new fabric unless it is a remnant on sale even from the sale price. I sit next to her, snipping buttons from an old shirt, tearing off seams and cuffs so there will be solid pieces for her to cut. I pick threads from the tiny holes of the buttons, "cleaning them up" so they can be strung and sent to the missions in Africa. The quilt, which will be a sunburst pattern, seems out of place in this dim room where one good light pools us in its moon, where corners blur with shadows. Wind pushes against the window glass like something trying to get in.

Women in my family have always made quilts. It is almost always winter work, the work of subzero nights when everything must stay interior because the cold will brook no outside work and little error. In my family, quilting is about goodness that comes of never wasting; it follows both the tenets of the church and the hard lessons of the Depression. It is a way to make something lovely out of very little. Quilting holds memory too, though we don't talk much about the way my Aunt's hands linger over certain patches, or her voice when she says, "This was your uncle's second best shirt, the one he wore on first and third Sundays." It is perhaps our only way to make the larger order out of the chaos of storms and whatever hard life is perking under the ice that caps our roofs.

In that storm where I am caught in a house that is never warm, it seems to me that piecing quilts is a way to keep things small. The little squares chafe with limits; the triangles look brief with boundaries. And for all that this quilt will be one of her brightest, it is not yet on the frame. I have no larger picture of how it will replicate the sun. Everything feels enclosed and pointed. Nothing opens, there is nothing of—the word would be *abundance*. I lift a sleeve and tug hard to rip off the cuff, but instead, tear it down the center in a strip too small to be used. I drop my hands in my lap.

Aunt Mary clears her throat again. "I think you're tired."

"I guess." I cannot tell her I want a river of warm water to play in.

"The spare room is pretty cold." I wait. "It's been closed all winter, you know."

I know the room. The north light leaks in like fog over the bed with its dark metal frame stacked with boxes of stored clothes that smell of old bodies and must.

She says, "You should sleep in my room. In the extra bed. It's a little warmer there."

She doesn't say the next thing, but I know. The sagging twin in her room is where my Uncle John slept. I will sleep in the bed of a dead man. I try not to think of this as I put down the scraps.

I get ready for bed in the cold bathroom, pulling on one of her big undershirts and keeping on my socks. When I return to her bedroom she is standing in a flannel nightgown she has made herself. It has long sleeves but no ruffles and no trim. It is thin with wear. On the metal chair near her window, her clothes are folded; her large bra rests, a rumpled egg, on top.

In the soft light I cannot help but see her body, how she is softer, rounder, without the trappings of the housedress. She catches me looking and says, "Say your prayers." I kneel at the edge of the bed, trying not to lean too hard onto it, trying not to disturb whatever of Uncle John is still there. She doesn't pray with me, but lets me make my silent prayers, my small Hail Marys and Our Fathers for my brothers and sisters, for good grades and for . . . what is it, a yearning without a question. And then I say three more Hail Marys that something bad will not happen because I am about to climb into Uncle John's bed.

When she sees me bless myself, she says, "Get in before your feet get cold."

My feet are already cold, but still I hesitate as I stand before the folded-back sheets. When I reach out, and despite the fact that there is some heat in this room, the stiff cotton feels cold. I pull the sheets back, my touch tentative on the yellowed fabric. I turn to her. She says, "There are no fleas."

Fleas aren't the problem.

When you are wading into cold water, there is a point in which you must get in, no matter what, you just have to dive under. It will hurt. It will make you scream. But you have to do it or you haven't been in. This feels like that.

With a flurry, I lift and tug and leap. I climb in and tuck my feet under and topple against the pillow. The springs squeak. I freeze. I am not to believe in ghosts. Then I realize what the sound is, a bed squeaking. I curl on my side toward her, alert in case it takes a while for Uncle John to know I am there.

She is pulling the pins out of her hair.

They are big, bronzy-colored pins with open prongs, not tight like bobby pins. She pulls a dozen from the braid wrapped around her head and places them in a small crystal bowl on the plain dresser. She lifts her heavy arms and pulls the braid away from its cap of hair and unwraps it from its circle. It falls heavily across her shoulder, an ash-colored snake curling over her breasts. There is no rubber band to unwind, simply the fine ends of gray hair that she lifts without looking. She unbraids quickly, pulling the three strands from their hold on one another. I watch as the braid comes undone, as the silver ropes come loose, opening so that the hair separates and spreads thickly on her shoulders. She works up toward her neck, raking her fingers down through the hair every few inches to keep it from tangling until finally it is a cinder-colored cascade of waves like hard rain. She picks up the wide paddle of her brush and pulls it through her hair. She brushes until the ripples settle, as though they were something too lush, something that must be trained to straightness.

I cannot take my eyes off what comes next.

She leans over and pulls all the hair forward so that it touches the floor in a silver waterfall. She brushes from the nape forward, pulling the hair down, brushing all its undersides. It shimmers, shivers in a long ripple of uncolor. It is like seeing the unraveling of a halo. I want to reach out and touch this thing that must have been what Uncle John saw every night, this silver wash that fills the room.

Is this why they had to pray so much?

With a soft fuff, she straightens up, catches me looking, and repeats my mother's time-worn command: "Don't stare." I pretend to close my eyes.

She pulls strands of hair from the brush and places it on the dresser. She kneels on the rag rug, crosses herself, leans against her sloping mattress and looks at the cross over her bed. She is praying as she always does, with her face firm as old and settled snow. I am watching the fall of silver hair, thick with . . . what it is? Unbraided, her hair is finally one abundant thing in this night. It shimmers with the afterburn of color, like charcoal at its hottest point, that cool gray-white color of ash that is impossible and dangerous to touch for its heat.

Something like a soul.

THE BLACK FAN

My mother is standing on the edge of the backyard, watching the heavy clouds scuttle across the sky. The men are hooking up equipment, slinging chains over their shoulders. The old windmill rises over us, its iron struts thrumming in the wind. Something is turning over, leaves in rain, color in fall. The people standing around the backyard mutter about the news, they talk about what Kennedy has said about the missiles. There is something called a crisis that my father has said is serious. My uncle laughs and says *prosperity is just around the corner* in the way he talks when he means the opposite. This wind has been blowing for days.

We are standing around the well-pit. Our old well was too shallow, the pressure too light, the pipes not properly insulated. A new well has been sunk and the pit has been widened so that a new pump can fit where the windmill pivots dropped like iron needles into the depths. The stone walls have been retucked. My father has said that it should stay dry down there now, if we ever have to get underground. And no one is using windmills to bring up their water anymore.

We watch the windmill. Its slow turning has been the longest song of my childhood, its metal wheel the oldest silhouette. Every sunny day I have watched that shadow move across the yard and over the roof of our house. The leggy tracing of its supports and struts shift, straight and clear, in and out of the kitchen window every morning that there is light. Different from the shadows of tree branches or laundry in wind, these have definition. And the windmill itself is something I can see from way down the road. It tells me my home is in place, like the pins Sister puts into maps to show us where the missions are. I can find shadows just like it on Uncle Joe's farm and on Ed Smith's and at Birkman's place.

The new pump's voice turns on and off depending on how much water we use. I hear the soft throb of the motor after Mom's second load of washing and Saturday night bath time. Although no longer needed, the windmill has stood, and every inch I have grown this fall, the low *creeeek* of its blades has accompanied, as though it is making the sound my silent bones cannot. My legs have grown longer with the long breath of steel turning in the wind. I hear its metal in the air like something speaking. I have always loved this tall thing, how it stands against the cold and the weathers that come sweeping over us like coarse sheets.

My father and Ed and Uncle Joe set up the welder. My father puts on the odd helmet that makes him look like a creature from Tom Swift stories. He bends to the arc that we have been told is too bright to look at directly. I look at my mother who is looking up at the rust and gray rays, the shape of a color wheel without the color. We hear the whine and hiss as they cut the struts, cut the L-shaped steel that holds up the circular blade that has graced our farm for decades.

My mother, with her auburn-gray hair and strong jaw, has too many faces today. One is proud, full of a dream I have heard her tell Dad, that she wants *something better* and the well will help. It is here, near the well-pit that she wants the new flower garden, here that she wants to set the pretty buckboard seat from the old school. But her face is also about the water jugs she filled just yesterday, twenty gallons stored in shelves in the basement. *Just in case, not to worry.*

I watch her face watching the windmill, listening to it comb the wind. She has said that *times change.* But my mother's eyes will miss what they see when she looks out the kitchen window in the morning. She sees already how the sky will look empty without it; she sees that the world will get lonelier.

When they have cut through three of the iron legs that stretch up some thirty-five feet, they hook up the tractor. They loop and tie the chains and ropes as high up as they can scramble. They turn a key and an engine's thud rises over the wind. My father shoves the tractor into gear. The tractor pulls; the chains straighten, grow taut. A few of the rusted stringers pop like gunshots. The men wave us back. But we do not go inside, we watch from the windy edge of the yard.

I think she is like a tall woman of dark bones with a black fan that moves in the wind. I think she is something that has watched over us. I think she is as old as a grandmother and as holy as church. She is leaving now. Times are changing.

The map of the world comes into our house every night now.

Her coming down happens slowly, with cold words. *Pull. Go. Stop. Go. Gun it. Go. Go.* They pull the structure east, away from the house. The steel shudders. The tractor labors but then moves steadily. The chains and ropes hold. The fourth leg, uncut, bends at the ankle, and controls the fall. The windmill begins to tremble, to keel, the top moving in a dark arc, this tallness that held our sky. It shifts, drawing its compass line across the low clouds. There is a slow squeal of metal so deep and strange I cannot look away. The structure moves through the air, and not until the last moments does weight carry it down, the steel bars thudding against the rutted yard so hard we can feel the impact in our feet, like faraway thunder. The blades clang against each other like metal feathers, then bend in half against the yellowed grass, folding up in disarray, trembling against earth now that they are out of the air where they have always belonged.

I thought it would have folded up into a compact thing like a paper fan decorated with small birds. We could simply have put it away then. But it is broken, each blade tangled against another, the bang and scrape still fluttering in the wind. The men swarm over the steel girders with the welder, cutting the dark supports into scrap metal, which they will sell.

They will keep the heavy struts to build a new asparagus picker.

My mother walks over to the well-pit and looks down. The new pump hums steadily, bringing up the water from inside the earth. The hired man is already digging out the footings that were buried outside the corners. She thanks him for his help. He nods. She steps forward, touches the spigot she will use to run the hoses for flowers. She looks at the skeleton of iron and frowns quietly. But her strong hands reach out, and she turns on the faucet. She lets it run into the grass, then bends and splashes her face with the fresh water, rinsing her skin with new water. She turns to me, gestures for me to do the same, and when I have done so—washed the dust and wet from my face—we look up to where the sky is now a wild empty blue except for the storm clouds coming in swiftly.

Harm

The houses of our bodies hold stories. Most are lost, shaping the way we are without our knowing why, but with some we can see how it is, how they return in certain weathers. I have three scars, three small stories of harm from growing up—one on my face, one on my knee, and one I do not speak of much because it is forgotten, though it aches in the right atmosphere. They are all linked by my need to move forward, sometimes blindly, by the momentum of my life.

The third scar happens while I am babysitting for neighbors. Here is another farmhouse in another township, another tattered living room with pieces of clothing, small metal tractors, dolls, shoes, and afghans scattered about the room. There are five children, more to come.

After their parents have left the house, after my little charges are tucked into the upstairs bedrooms, the hired hand—I'll call him Will—comes to the house. He has finished milking in the barn. He is hungry so I get him something to eat. We sit at the table and pretend to talk farming. How many cows he milked. How many tons of cherries will be harvested. How many acres he plowed, though I know the owner does the plowing. We talk with the voices of authority we hear in our parents' voices. I like this. I feel older, more adult. It feels like pretending to be married. He is in his late teens, maybe back from a short stint in the service, out of high school, and not good looking, but I don't know that yet. I chatter, wanting to be friendly, wanting him to like me, wanting him to appreciate me in some way I can't even say yet.

I wash some dirty dishes. Babysitters are valued more if they do the dishes, though they don't get paid more for it. Sometimes I do the dishes, sometimes I don't; I do them tonight. I think this makes me look good. We talk. He seems to want to talk. He says he has a headache. I think about what to do about this problem. After a while, I tell him I will look for aspirin.

I am peering into the metal medicine cabinet with the squeaking mirror door. When I close the door he is there, behind me, looking into the mirror over my shoulder, standing very close to me.

I realize that something may happen like what I have read about in some of the magazines my grandmother has. Magazines like *True Confessions*. I have begun to dream about boys. I have recently realized that the kissing of my elementary grades was what it was supposed to be, a kind of play. There is something more real out there in the world of women and men. I am curious yet cautious, and now, after the years in the church's teachings, way too afraid. I slide sideways out of the room. In the doorway, I turn and say, "I don't think they have any aspirin."

I walk back into the living room and turn on the TV. He comes out of the bathroom. We watch TV for a while. I think he told me it was his birthday. Yes, there is talk about birthdays, his birthday. I ask him how his headache is. He says it's worse. His voice racks a little. I say I'll look again for the aspirin, and go back into the bathroom.

Why do I go back to look again? If I answer one way, he is manipulating a girl who wants to please so he can take advantage of her. If I answer it another way, I am making my first simple advances. But I think it is me spinning forward. I think it is the way I must run down the hill, down the stairs, into the next hard thing. It is how I become who I am.

I don't know how he came to be kissing me, or how I came to be squirming under his arms, forced against the bathroom wall. To this day I don't know, and I couldn't tell if it was one time or a hundred times I pursed my lips to keep his tongue from entering my mouth. I don't think I succeeded. I remember feeling his tongue. I remember ending up on the floor. I am quite sure my jeans were never off, but do I remember adjusting my waistband? I remember the feeling that it shouldn't be happening, that I couldn't stop it. It was all wrong.

For the first time in all the things I have remembered about my life, it is important not to add the deduced detail, not to follow the logical progression between two points—if I remember this moment and that moment, then this other moment must have happened in between. Given that memory can be a cloud in the wind, I will not say anything but what I know.

I know that something happened, but I also understand—and I say this with absolute honesty—that I cannot remember the whole story. And in that there is a kind of gift.

What happens afterward is clearer. The neighbors drop me off in the driveway. I enter our house through the mudroom, walk through the large dining room that always smells of food and burned coffee, and into the quieter living room. I sit on a chair at the bottom of the staircase, rub my saddle shoes on the green shag carpet my father has picked out just this year, our first carpeting. I wait for my parents to come out of the bathroom, where they are washing up, to say good night. I know what I must say. I must say it now.

What goodness allowed me that?

But the telling is not simple. I sit pushing my feet forward and back on the carpet. I say a small prayer. The prayer is about my mother. I know that she is confused by who I am. I know she has been relieved by my interest in school, the church, by my happiness with Mrs. Smith's attention, by the arrangement with Aunt Mary. But she also knows, in ways I do not understand, that I have made up whole tales without a stitch of fact. She knows I have fibbed to her about boys, about work I have not done. She knows I love the drama of the world. She tolerates little of it. Will she believe me now?

She comes out of the bathroom, wiping her face with a worn towel.

"Mom," I look up from the floor. I feel as though I am floating above the green shag. A huge distance forms, like in a science fiction movie, when the spaceship takes off. Everything is rushing away. I feel cold and shaky. The words halt out one at a time, "Mom, can I talk . . . to you?"

Throughout her life her instincts have created survival from disaster for her family. That instinct kicks in now, fast and hard. She sees my face, and I see hers. She puts the towel on her shoulder. She sits down on the edge of the couch. She takes on that calmness that says *nothing can be out of control, nothing can be rushed.* Everything will be safe, and all that is wrong will be taken care of. She is making time for me to talk to her. She loves me. Will she hear the truth?

"Tonight, Will came to the house with a headache . . ." I stop. Waiting. Her face has changed after all; like the breaking surface of a quiet river. I take a breath, listening to how her voice will sound. It trembles a little when she calls softly to my father, "John, you'd better come . . ." There is no question in it.

My mother and father never doubted me as I answered questions down to the new word I learn, the one with the hard "p" that pops the breath at the end.

No, he did not rape me.

I know that I told them carefully what did happen. I cannot remember what I said. I can remember afterward.

In the way of people who prefer to handle trouble on their own, things are taken care of. Some time later, Will leaves the area.

My mother is careful but not caught up. For a while, she listens to me sleep at night. She watches. And then, as the strange reserve, the tightness that had entered my body leaves me, and my girl-ways come swimming back, she makes sure every day is like it is supposed to be. Routine slowly takes on its normal light and shadow, all its daily harvests. The moment fades and crumbles like tattered paper. Once or twice she asks if I think about what he did. I tell her no, and in fact I do not.

I learn to forget. This is what she did for me. She believed me. As did my father. And then she made my world ordinary. They said, in daily tasks, in routine bedtimes, in everything they did, *Look, Look, this house will hold you. It will tuck you in and keep you safe.* Like soldiers mending from battle I am allowed to forget. And I do. It is no small gift.

So why tell such a broken and fragmented story at all? Having forgotten it, what is inside that needs to be passed into language? Into light? Years later I know what helped me first is that I told them immediately. Some pain drifted out of the moment just by saying the words. I did not know words could lose their weight like that. That may be one reason to keep this story.

The other, more telling reason may have been that, in light of what we know now of incidents like this for young girls, in light of everything that could have infected that moment, they did the things that allowed me to leave the small, tight-cornered room of fear and shame. They listened. She listened. They did not doubt. They diffused fear by surrounding me with the oldest law of tribal family—that of protection. And then, though they paid attention, they didn't make it the center of my life. They let me sleep; they let me learn other things.

The people of my childhood would say *no harm done.*

Still I go back to the memory in all its scattered pieces. After a long time, I discover that what remains is the unexpected. I was moving forward and came up hard against the wall, the corner, the floor. One day I know, I was wounded by the abruptness, not of motion, but the way it turned into its opposite.

That someone would do that. The violence of surprise, the surprise of violation.

Slowly I realize, despite my blatant curiosity about the body, sex, and all that goes with it, how long it takes me to trust a boy kissing me. I wonder if something hasn't happened to my mouth. Not any other part of my body, just my mouth. I am always afraid of some pressure, something forced about the tongue. I am not sure if it is there, and yet it is there, a scar without an image—harm done.

THE NAME

I am at the oak table; my mother is at the sewing machine, its beetle body humming in little bursts and starts. I am hemming the beautiful plaid satin skirt my mother has sewn from lucky remnants, three pieces of pure indulgence, enough so that each daughter can have one elegant skirt. Although she has grumbled about how we will never appreciate them, how we will dirty the skirts before we get home from church, I can tell she is proud to make them. And unlike washing dishes, which is often one long battle, hemming is something I like to do. It is not in two parts. It is not washing and drying. It is me and the needle and the fabric and the circle of the skirt. It comes around to where you started. Not like the rest of the world with its strange fads, the Beatles, the new president and his pretty wife, the hula hoop. And there is this thing called a cold war that could cause a real war that I am so afraid of that I wake at night with its nightmare in my head.

In my real life, my mother sends me to Aunt Mary who makes me breakfast and prays but does not teach me what prayer is. The sisters teach me science and history, and to do good, but doing good remains mysterious no matter that they make us memorize a list of good works. Mrs. Smith teaches me art and beauty but talks of nature and color, not the body. Summer comes and there is more talk of a war on the other side of the planet, and my father remembers his own war, though he keeps its secrets. My mother worries all the time but she sews us skirts and keeps the world from rocking. All these things bump into one another like too many cups in a cupboard.

But while hemming, I forget time, though I do not yet understand why that is a pleasure. We are in the dining room, my mother finishing the waistband on Marijo's skirt. She is bending over the machine, preparing to run the box pleats under the presser foot threaded with green. The light comes in through the west window and falls on the fabric. It glows but her hands are absorbed and quick. She does not look up. In a moment she will call tall Marijo to come in from picking beans to see if the band fits. I sit at the table, holding the cloth over the oak grain, bending too. I glance sideways at her, but mostly I am looking at my stitches, at how the loop of thread invisibly ties one part of fabric to another.

I ask, "What do you pray for?"

She has pins in her mouth but she takes them out and slips them into the tomato cushion. "I pray for all of you."

"Do you like it?"

"I pray. God hears. It's not about liking."

"How do you know he hears?"

"None of you have died."

She releases the presser foot. It snaps down, a short tight sound. "What's this about?"

"Nothing."

I want to tell her it's about the mama cat who abandoned her kittens, about how I don't like to babysit anymore, about the way I want to touch my skin, about how I want to understand Aunt Mary's rosary and the way she unbraids her hair. About jealousy and shame and trying to understand the news we watch at night. It is about feeling alone, which I do not yet know is ordinary. It's about how the circle of the skirt is empty inside. It's about feeling far away from the fields.

"Have you chosen yet?" she asks, changing the subject, and pulling me back into the world where I belong. She picks up a thread, loops it around the foot, and breaks it.

"What?" I am not sure where she is headed, though I suspect it has something to do with the church since prayer always leads to that.

"Your confirmation name. You have to decide soon. The sisters are compiling the list for the bishop."

I have, though I haven't said yet. Do I know already what will happen? I watch my little silver needle. I hem the skirt. "I'd like to choose Rose."

She looks up. "Rose?" There is a lot of *why* in her voice.

I am remembering my favorite saint.

"She was the girl who laughed at Satan. She lived in Peru and she was weak and sick, but when Satan appeared to her, all fierce and scary, she laughed at him and he went away. I really like that story."

My mother turns the kind of quiet that is prickly with decision. She has something to say and she is getting ready to say it.

"It's not a family name."

Was it supposed to be? I think about this. I remember that she has suggested, more than once, that I look among family names for my confirmation name.

"It's the name of a flower, something that grows." I am thinking this might be a way to argue for my choice. Farmers grow things. But I can feel already that this will not go the way I hoped. "We have those seven sister roses in the back yard. So that will remind me." I say with false confidence.

My mother, with her sure sense of detecting the manure of rationalizing, sniffs and says, "You've never paid attention to the roses before."

"Well, I could start."

She's had enough. "That's not the point. The point is that it would mean a lot if you chose a family name."

It will do me little good to argue. "Whose name?"

"Well, there's Catherine, your godmother's name." Aunt Catherine is my father's sister. But I can tell by the way my mother has said this without a big push: this is not the name she's really headed for. She is leading to another carefully, like picking raspberries from a prickly branch. "And there's Julia, your grandmother's name."

Oh.

"Grandma Julia?"

"She'd like that, you know." My mother speaks through pins in her mouth.

I know Grandma would like me to choose her name but I don't like it. It's my grandmother's name, for heaven's sake. My aunt's is no better. It is precisely because they are family names that I am not interested. I want something like the girl who laughed at evil, something brave and unrelated to the solid folks of my life. Silently, I review the list of saints I know something about. I run through the names of all the lives I've read. The needle goes still in my hands. "It's supposed to be a saint who means something to us. I don't know any Saint Julia. Is there one?"

She takes offense. "Your Grandma Julia was baptized in the Catholic Church so she has to have a saint's name." A pause, another nudge. "You could look up Saint Julia."

"Okay, but I like Rose."

My mother sighs and gets up, moving quickly now, already thinking about the next meal. "I don't want to push you, but I think you know it would mean a lot to your grandmother if you took her name for confirmation."

I put the skirt down and stare out the window. In the way only Michigan can, it has changed, now dulled with shadow. Light, then dark; clear, then clouds. I remember my Grandma. I like her a lot. I like her curly white-white hair like a halo. I remember her stocky body, the sway from her bad knee. I remember how she stands on the small porch of her house and waves good-bye from under the trumpet vines. She crochets and tats beautiful doilies and sells them. She is my mother's mother, a figure who lives with us in winter because it is too hard to be alone over there in Elbridge Township, too hard to get to the Mission church. She gives me money on my birthday. She makes the best fried potatoes.

It would be good to pick her name. But . . .

I try out the names, placing the confirmation name after the given name. *Anne-Marie Julia Oomen. Anne-Marie Rose Oomen.* To me, there is no comparison. It is about the music, the way the O's work together.

"I like the sound of Rose," I say.

"This is not about the sound." Her voice rises a bit. "It's not about you. It's about your faith. And honoring your grandmother." Then, knowing how direct commands can trigger my defiance, she says more quietly. "You think about it." And she leaves the room to find out where the beans are.

I put the skirt down. I sneak into the living room where on the bookshelf under the staircase there is a black book called a missal that has fourteen hundred pages with the gospels, epistles, the liturgy for every day. It lists the saints' days with short descriptions of their lives. I flip through pages thin as leaves after winter. I find the tiny print about Saint Julia. I read and sigh. Although miracles are attributed to her, she lived her life in a convent and did not speak for most of her life except to her confessor. She took a vow of silence.

A vow of silence? What is my mother thinking?

I walk slowly back to the skirt and touch the plaids, tracing the colors first one way, then another. It's true, there are silences in me I do not understand. What if I gave them to God, in this naming thing called confirmation? But it doesn't ring true. These are my silences, where words are born, where reading comes from, where my world comes to stillness both raucous and mysterious. I hold the plaid fabric and look out at the yard. I remember my grandmother's face and how she and my mother glance at each other, how they talk on the phone with voices that are close to each other, like when animals sleep close together in a cold barn. I remember how in winter when she lives with us, my mother will stop folding laundry or ironing clothes and go to Grandma's room and sit still for a while. I remember how my mother, who has so little time to laugh, laughs with Grandma Julia.

I trace the plaid, a green stripe one way, blue another. I would like to laugh with my mother. Her laugh is as silky as this fabric, rare and lovely. I sit down and make the stitches as small as I can, folding the hem up into the underside of the skirt, trying to keep the length even all the way around. When she comes in with Marijo and the beans, I tell her it will be *Julia.* She nods, touches my shoulder, and says I am doing a good job on that hem. While she snips the beans, I pull the thread until the circle comes around to where it began and I never tell her how I love the other name.

HOUSE OF FIELDS

It is Sunday Mass. I am tired; I feel that kind of looseness in my body that I feel more and more often, like nothing is connected to anything else. I have not slept again, then slept too hard in the late hours of the morning and so waking is like picking stones out of a dry field, that kind of work. But the family goes to church on a hot July Sunday bright with green. We climb out of the car, Rick takes Patti's hand, though she's ready to start school now. Mom touches Marijo's shoulder. Tom walks near Dad. I trail, staring out at the fields, until my mother turns and I hurry to catch up. She does not like to be late.

We enter church through the tall paneled doors, propped open for the air. Midsummer light spills in from outside in a square block down the wide center aisle. It is a distinct light, sharp and bright, and every person who moves through it casts a dark shadow as they step into the church. Coming from the bright light of the parking lot or the road, it is as though we enter night when we pass through it. The light shapes a short tunnel leading inward to the church, then ceases so abruptly that many halt next to the holy water font, peering toward the ghost of an altar, thinking there is no light at all. Then our eyes adjust, and shadows take on shape.

I dip my hand in the stale water, bless myself, and move toward the darkness, noticing how the in-church air cools the heat of the July morning. I genuflect and move into the pew where our family sits every Sunday. Behind me, I feel light flicker as people move in and out of these two pools. I am curious about the light, so I turn around and watch as a stooped woman with a cane steps over the threshold. She nearly disappears in the brightness, a two-legged darkness moving forward in the light. Her form stops at the door, wavering. One of the ushers, a young man in an ill-fitting sports jacket, steps forward, takes her by the arm, and leads her until her eyes adjust to the quieter light in the church. She pats his arm. A rosary is tangled in her arthritic hands.

It is Aunt Mary. But she is old. It races through me. How did that happen? When did she start to use a cane. How could I not have noticed?

My mother watches too. I see her turn toward the light and look at Aunt Mary's form. I see a soft acknowledgment in her attention, a quiet acceptance of what is. I watch Aunt Mary and my mother face the quieter lights of the church.

I turn again toward the door. They come, in families or alone, dressed in a pretty dress, a good shirt. Greiners, VanderZandens, Vanden Heuvels, Lipps, Kokx, Dennerts, Lathrops, Daleys, Brays, Hammerles, Malburgs. Others whose names I do not know but my parents would. They could tell me the family histories. But as they enter, each person momentarily disappears, becomes less formed, surrounded by a nimbus of light, then reappears as who they are, and we know each other. I pay attention now, and realize that no one looks, in everyday life, quite like they look once inside the church. They are better dressed, yes, but that is not what I am seeing. I think they are also smaller, even the big men who, on other days lift, haul, shout, and plow, even they look softer, something harsh gone out of their faces. Who they are is laid bare for a moment. It is a look that, if the men could see it they would fear, for it would remind them of weakness. Most of the women would know it is how belief works to keep us humble. I turn and watch George and Elsie, Marie and Hank, Tom and Marge, Melvin and Phyllis, Bud and Judy. Little Lisa and Bernice and Jane. And in the shadow of stained glass, I realize: *we are all here.*

Joe and Theta herd their lanky children with soft nudges. Monica Hammerle's mother emerges from the light with a green hat. I see Mrs. Smith and her husband walk the aisle all the way to the front where they sit before the statue of Saint Joseph. I see an altar boy leave the sacristy, walk down a side aisle, and ask another boy to come serve. I hear my brothers and sisters scuffling against the kneeling benches. We disappear, like something gone, and reappear, ourselves but different. And I can smell them too, a mother's floral cologne, a father's sharp aftershave, the hints of manure and sweet milk, and sometimes the hints of a shirt worn one too many times to Sunday Mass without being laundered. And something else here too—the scent of how we smell under soap or sweat. Oh, our dreams and the old, old sorrows.

And here is a soft chorus of fabric and shoes, of purses being snapped and unsnapped, hymnal pages being turned, old people coughing and the soft coo of a young mother soothing a baby, the giggle of little boys about to tie someone's shoes together. I listen to Mr. Franks, a man with dark hair slicked with a lot of Vitalis, sing the Gloria in an operatic baritone. I listen to a hundred people brush against the hard-polished wood of the pews as they stand and sit and kneel together. I listen and stare at these people, for once facing the same direction. All of it echoes, a second language under the liturgy, sounds made of both light and the mundane, one thing meaning the other.

It comes to me slowly. Everyone can be recognized, named, by their bodies, the sound and look and smell.

The Sanctus rings *Holy, holy, holy,* the consecration rings with chimes, *This is my body.*

This is my body?

In that moment I hear it differently, my mind finding fields of meaning in the words. This is my body, our bodies. Is this what is meant?

Is this how it is really? Is this why I love the wash of Aunt Mary's hair brushed in the night light more than the rosary, why I love the sound of Mrs. Smith's laugh more than the color wheel? Why I love my mother and father's touch more than their direction?

The light shifts, heat rises in my face.

Is this blasphemy?

It doesn't feel that way.

It feels like learning. It feels like opening a book. It feels attached to something. I look around, back to that spill of light.

Is that it? I am attached to all of this, to them, because I have a body. I am like them, of them. I am of this house, the house that is a body inside another house that is a family, a people, all of us.

I run my fingers over my palm, I fold my hands and feel the hollow space between the palms. Is grace a hollow like the bowl of your palm, like a small darkness surrounded by skin? Maybe emptiness is the only grace we know, who we are but we are together in it. I sit in some kind of dangerous prayer, not as one who is asking for something, but one who is thinking. Thinking.

It closes in on me. I feel dizzy with it, with not being able to bear knowing. I rise, whisper to my mother that I need some air. She looks at me intently for a moment, then lets me go and turns back to the Mass. I walk toward the back of the church. I walk through the blaze, into the ordinary sunlight, out to where I can feel heat drifting over the fields, where the fields spread out around this house of God as they do around our own farmhouse, as they do around each house of every family who lives on this road, on this land. This too is a house, this open space, these fields, and I, for a moment, am of it. Perhaps more than of the house I have just left. This is the one that allows the mind to stretch out, to discover in the face of loss and grace that there is still more to know. I breathe deeply until I am steady. I walk across the street, out into a wheat field full of grain and sun and crows and the old, old wideness of the world. I walk until I am ready to return to what I must learn next.